DERRILL CORBIN

MADE TO

RESPONDING BOLDLY AND TENACIOUSLY TO JESUS' CALL ON YOUR LIFE

MOVE

Acorn &
Oak Press

MANNAHOUSE
RESOURCE

Portland, Oregon

Made to Move
© 2024 Derrill Corbin

Published by Acorn & Oak Press
in collaboration with Mannahouse Resources
mannahouseresource.com
Portland, Oregon

An imprint of Grafo House Publishing
Tulsa, OK | Guadalajara, Mexico

ISBN   978-1-963127-12-6 (paperback)
        978-1-963127-12-6 (eBook)

To contact the author or inquire about bulk discounts for churches and study groups, visit mannhouseresource.com.

Printed in the United States of America
27 26 25 24   1 2 3 4

I would like to dedicate this book to my wife, Michal.
You are a rockstar, a woman of great faith,
indisputable character, and a pioneer leader
and culture builder in your own right.
You live the truths I've outlined in this book.
I'm challenged and made better by you.

PRAISE FOR *MADE TO MOVE*

"The best books come from the heart of the author: their life experiences of living through storms, breaking under disappointments, and finding pathways to overcoming. *Made to Move* is the heart of the author put into words. It's biblical, emotional, insightful, practical, and real. I believe the reader will be impacted and motivated to move forward into God's best. Well done, Pastor Derrill Corbin!"
—*Dr. Frank Damazio, Chairman, Ministers Fellowship International*

"I've spent the last fifteen years exploring and dreaming about what authentic Gospel movements look like in cities around the world. Where churches are united around seeking the shalom of the places where God has carried them. Where many are responding to the Good News as it's clearly lived out and boldly shared. My friend Derrill Corbin has given us an important resource in *Made to Move*, for it's impossible to see the renewal we seek at the macro level without seeing individuals moving closer to God, to each other, and toward the world we seek to reach. This practical book is just what we need, and I'm confident God will use it to shape us into the image of Christ."
—*Kevin Palau, President, Luis Paua Association*

"*Made to Move* is a powerful testament to living out God's call with boldness, tenacity, and purpose. Having walked closely with Derrill for almost three decades, I can attest that this book encapsulates his life message and passion for movement in Christ. He not only preaches these principles but exemplifies them in every aspect of his life. I have the deepest love and respect for Derrill and believe him to be one of the most trustworthy, exemplary leaders I know, and I am confident this book will inspire and challenge you to embrace the journey God has set before you to become one on the move."
—*Marc Estes, CEO & Co-Founder, VisitorReach*

"In his latest work, Pastor Derrill masterfully unveils a concept that is crucial not only to our spiritual growth but also to our financial well-being. The core message is clear: we were not merely made to move; we were made to grow. Movement is essential to growth and trade, and without trade, there can be no growth or progress. This book is a must-read for anyone eager to unlock their potential and the potential of those they lead. All economic progress begins with movement, while stagnation leads to regression and poverty. Having worked with entrepreneurs and marketplace leaders for over twenty-five years, I can attest to the critical role of movement in both the marketplace and in leadership at large."
—*Patrice Tsague, CEO and Co-Founder; Nehemiah Entrepreneurship Community and Smart Oregon Solutions Inc.*

"Emphatically...WOW!! Derrill Corbin has masterfully crafted a life manual that is practical, achievable, rich, and inspiring. *Made to Move* is not a book just for a leader or a layman, it is for everyone. And the simplicity of Derrill's impartation will clearly help everyone transition their existence from the stress of the 'doing' to the delight of the 'being.' I encourage everyone to get this book and hear the God-Whisper for your life wellness!"
—*Howard Rachinski, Founder, Christian Copyright Licensing International (CCLI) and Co-Founder, VisitorReach*

Change is inevitable. Sometimes it's slow and evolutionary, and sometimes it's fast and revolutionary. In this season of revolutionary and disruptive change in every realm of society all around the world, the Lord is calling His Church globally to embrace the necessity of enacting revolutionary, transformational change as well. One of the biggest changes we need is for our churches to embrace biblical movement dynamics rather than Western corporate growth models. Derrill's book couldn't be more timely nor more spot-on in its message. It's a fantastic first step into understanding movement dynamics for any Christian or church who wants to understand the times and know what to do about them, just like the sons and daughters of Issachar in 1 Chronicles 12:32. It's a must read!
—*Fred Markert, Missions Team, Church of the Highlands*

CONTENTS

SECTION 3: THE FUNDAMENTALS OF MOVEMENT

SECTION 4: ADVANCING JESUS' MOVEMENT

FOR THE ONES WHO MOVE

People ask me from time to time, "What is the most difficult thing that you face in leadership?" In my experience, people are often expecting me to say, "making large financial decisions," "speaking in front of large crowds," or "leading an organizationally complex church." There are probably a hundred things people would expect me to say. But the answer that comes from my core is "unmet potential."

When I see a young person settle and not pursue a dream, it tears at my heart. When a couple is stuck in generational poverty and the pathway out seems so daunting that they freeze and maintain course, I grieve. When a prophetic word stirs an entire congregation and then they settle back into routine, I wonder what could have been had they pressed through the discomfort. I have lost sleep over scenarios like this.

I've come to the conclusion that if the people of God could understand movement at its most basic level, we could break past barriers and fulfill the original purpose and divine design for our lives. Unmet potential might no longer grieve my soul. And then, if a community of 100, 200, or 5,000 could believe this together, a gospel movement that changes cities and nations could be born.

This dream is not rooted in a form of manifest destiny that is conspiring to take over the world one follower at a time (although I'd be lying if I said I wasn't intrigued by a good cult documentary from time to time). It is rooted in a deeply held belief that the Church that Jesus is building is meant to be powerful, to be on-mission, and to carry the good news to the ends of the earth, discipling nations and baptizing in the name of the Father, Son, and Holy Spirit.

I do think there is often a miss in the way so many of us have approached the idea of a gospel movement. We place far too much emphasis on what happens on platforms and in large crowds. The church's ministry and movement is measured by what happens in a weekend service. But that is not necessarily a true movement, really. It's a crowd. It's an assembly. It could be (don't get me wrong) a reflection of a gospel movement. But it's possible that thousands of people assemble, while few are on the move.

For an authentic gospel movement to be born, individuals must be faithfully on the move. They should be continually moving closer to God, closer to each other, and closer to the world around them. They are a collection of individuals who are taking daily steps toward a common righteous cause. They face obstacles and barriers, and they are even sideswiped by the world, the flesh, and the devil at times, but they do not stop.

This kind of movement is like leaven in a lump of dough. It's silent and may not be visible, but its effect is powerful and evident over time. It's not centered around a star; rather it's known for deference and honor among all. It's found in boardrooms, neighborhoods, and around kitchen tables.

To see this happen, there must be a shift.

> From **bigger** to **better**.
> From **crowd** to **disciples**.
> From **platform** to **table**.
> From **star** to **servant**.
> From **power** to **humility**.
> From **control** to **stewardship**.
> From **managers** to **shepherds**.
> From **entertainment** to **mission**.
> From **sermons** to **equipping**.
> From **seating** to **sending**.
> From **enterprise** to **movement**.

My dream in writing this book is to awaken who you were really meant to be. You were not created to be stuck, limited by your past, or bound in generational poverty. You were not created to sit in a large crowd, alone and detached from kingdom purpose.

You were created in the image of God. And God not only moves, he is movement. If this book could help you shift to become more like him and act like him, then my time writing it was worth every hour. Because I did not write it for me—I wrote it for you.

Let's move.

MOVEMENT IS GOD'S IDEA

The Spirit of God was hovering over the waters.

Genesis 1:2

Those who do not move, do not notice their chains.

—Rosa Luxemburg

Chapter 1

CREATED TO MOVE

One spring afternoon a few years ago, I was stuck—not spiritually, emotionally, or in any lofty way—but literally: a tractor I had borrowed from my father was buried to the axles in cement-like mud. Any attempt to go forward or even reverse only spun and dug deeper.

We lived in a rural area surrounded by forestland and had a beautiful year-round creek that ran by our house. The house was uninhabitable when we purchased the property, and the creek was overgrown in briars and brush. I grew up on a farm, so I'm not inept around heavy equipment (although I realize this story doesn't inspire much confidence). I knew I could use my dad's tractor and a large, attached mower to overcome the mountain of thorns and recover the beauty that I was confident lay underneath. I just hadn't banked on the mud. No pun intended.

I sat on the tractor seat for a while, staring grimly at the mess I'd made and with waves of angst rolling over me, trying to figure out what to do next. I'm pretty sure I didn't swear, but I certainly felt like it.

Eventually, though, I came up with a solution. I retrieved a large wooden beam I'd saved from the remodeling project on our house and laid it flat on the solid ground underneath the tractor beside the creek. I swiveled the tractor's bucket over to the beam and pushed down on it with the hydraulic strength of the tractor. The beam was strong and the ground stable, so the downward force slowly forced the tractor's front wheels upward. With careful maneuvering, I used the bucket and beam to gain enough traction to get out of the mess and back to solid ground. I never did live down that episode with my father, but at least I got the tractor out!

I've often thought back to that event. I've even used it in a sermon or two because it illustrates the importance of movement so vividly. I needed to conquer the overgrown mess of briars and bring back the lush beauty hidden beneath. But in my eagerness to solve the problem, I ended up getting so stuck that my own movement ceased. It took creativity, tenacity, and a little bit of desperation to solve the issue, and that solution involved (you guessed it) more movement.

> Movement is hard-wired into the human experience. It's part of who we are.

How would you define the human experience? What words would you choose to paint a picture of your life? I think of words like challenge, achievement, pain, grit, grace, and redemption. These ideas are at the core of what it means to be human; they are part of our individual story and etched into the collective history of humanity. And at their core, they are all stories of movement.

Movement is hard-wired into the human experience. It's part of who we are. It's impossible to conceive of this world or our place in it without movement.

On a physical level, movement is essential to life. Try living without a beating heart or expanding lungs. If we're not moving, we're dead!

Movement is intrinsic to all aspects of life—or at least it should be if we are going to live healthy lives. Without the emotional movement of reaching out or responding to others, friends are never made and relationships die. Without intellectual movement, our opinions fossilize and our ability to reason decays. Without evangelistic movement, the kingdom of God never expands. Without spiritual movement, our relationship with God withers.

I'm convinced that understanding movement's role in our lives is vital to experiencing all God has for us. God's calling and purpose for our lives are unique and personal. His thoughtfulness and design are specific to every single one of us to the point that he knows exactly how many hairs are on each of our heads. When we respond to his plan, he will infuse all we do with divine grace and energy.

You are called. By God himself. For a purpose.

If you answer that call—if you have the courage and perseverance to respond to its challenge—you will find a life worth living.

Your yes will be the starting point for movement. Spiritually, emotionally, physically, financially, and sometimes even geographically, movement will be required.

The good news is that movement comes naturally to us. The bad news is that quitting does too. Perhaps the most subtle hindrance to movement is the gravitational pull of everyday life. Inertia sets in as struggles, limitations, difficult people, emotional fatigue, financial challenges, and spiritual dryness make movement feel exhausting. Rarely, if ever, does meaningful movement occur without a few obstacles blocking the way. It's tempting to let those obstacles deflect us onto an easier path or cause us to stop completely.

But it doesn't have to end that way. In the following chapters, my goal is to help you understand how to respond to God's personal call, find purpose in every aspect of your daily life, overcome the inevitable obstacles with courage and grace, and live in the fullness God intends for you. In short, I want you to know that you were made to move...

> Closer to God.
> Closer to each other.
> Closer to the world around you.

We were not built to live stuck and without traction, merely staying still. Our default setting is movement: progress, creation, development, success. It's the way you and I were wired by our creator. This truth cannot be minimized or simply passed over when we read the first pages of Genesis.

> Then God said, "Let us make human beings in our image, to be like us. They will reign over the fish in the sea, the birds in the sky, the livestock, all the wild animals on the earth, and the small animals that scurry along the ground."
> So God created human beings in his own image.
> In the image of God he created them;
> male and female he created them.
> (Genesis 1:26–27 NLT)

Notice four things:

> **We were made by God**. God is the progenitor of humanity.
> **We were made to be with God**. God extended his family to include those he created.
> **We were made like God**. God is the model, pattern, and image of humanity.
> **We were made for God**. God established the eternal purpose for humanity.

Something deep inside us not only dreams of a better world but feels compelled to take action to achieve it. And while trauma, betrayal, grief, and a host of other forces work overtime in an attempt to get us stuck, that is not the future God has for us. The gravitational pull that leads us to a state of inertia is the effect of the fall on humanity. We were made for more than that. We're so convinced this is true that we've made the statement "Made for More!" the tagline of Portland Bible College, my alma mater, and where I still serve as chancellor.

A God Who Moves

We are hardwired for movement because God made us in his image and movement is part of who he is.

The Bible says that before creation, God's Spirit was "hovering" over the earth. The Hebrew term used here appears elsewhere in the Bible and in similar ancient languages, and it usually refers to the movement of a bird soaring in the air or stretching its wings over its nest to stir up its offspring to caringly and intentionally release their full potential.

God was not content to simply exist as some ethereal, formless, and purposeless being; he moved.

And God's movement wasn't aimless. The very first verse of the Bible says that God created, forming the earth, sky, and everything in them out of nothing. God created Adam and Eve and called them into a relationship with him. They walked together in the Garden, moving throughout creation and dreaming together of continual expansion of the garden's borders, eventually covering the whole earth. When Adam and Eve moved away from God by deliberately disobeying, God set in motion his plan of redemption to bring them back.

The rest of the Bible is the story of a God who moves, calling humanity back into relationship and purpose with him. The turning point of history was when God himself came down to earth as a human, walking among us both to give us an example of how to live and also to die in our place.

Humans move because we are made in the image of a God who is constantly moving. No wonder human history is a continual story of moving, creating, growing, and inventing. Even the violence and suffering we see are caused more often than not by a sin-twisted version of that same yearning for movement and growth.

We just can't help it. We are created to move.

The Lie of Busyness

We live in a society that almost worships productivity. On Amazon alone, there are over fifty thousand books devoted to the subject, and "life hacks" meant to help you get more done in less time are easy to find on YouTube (which, ironically, is a great way to get absolutely nothing done for the rest of the afternoon). American jobs, on average, offer the second-lowest number of paid vacation days of any country in the entire world. Unlike many developed nations, we don't guarantee paid leave. And over half of Americans who do get paid vacation days are so tied to their work that they don't even use them all.[1]

As a result of our culture's fixation on productivity, we seem compelled to be active all the time. Whether juggling projects at work, playing Whac-A-Mole with chores at home, or shuttling kids to more events than our pre-parenthood selves would have thought possible, our lives are often defined by busyness. Even vacations get tightly scheduled with "must-see" sights and activities we feel compelled to experience.

> I believe that answering God's call to move actually brings rest to our spirits, even while it gently demands action.

But busyness isn't movement. At least, it's not movement in the way I'm suggesting that God intends for us to move. I actually think it is one of the biggest barriers to movement because it deceives us into thinking we are already moving. We are doing so many things, and we are chronically exhausted, so surely we must be moving, right?

Well, no. The most tired I ever get while swimming is when I tread water. Busyness doesn't equate to forward movement.

My purpose in this book is not to make you busier. None of us has time for that. I believe that answering God's call to move actually brings rest to our spirits, even while it gently demands action. Jesus put that call this way: "Come to me, all who labor and are heavy laden, and I will give you rest. Take my yoke upon you, and learn from me, for I am gentle and lowly in heart, and you will find rest for your souls. For my yoke is easy, and my burden is light" (Matthew 11:28–30, ESV).

Can you imagine what those words must have sounded like to weary laborers toiling under the heat of the Middle Eastern sun? I can because they sound the same to me: like water to my thirsty soul.

Movement, God's Way

The kind of movement God intended isn't frantic busyness. It's natural, unforced, and filled with divine empowerment called grace. Is there an activity you perform well in? Maybe it's a sport, or music, or preaching, or building something, or balancing a spreadsheet. Doing it sometimes feels almost effortless, even though it's taking all your focus and strength. You feel fully alive—as if you were doing exactly what you were made to do. And it's glorious.

I'm not suggesting all of life will feel effortless. It won't. But I do think we can learn to trade in our frantic busyness for the "unforced rhythms of grace," as Eugene Peterson paraphrases the passage I just quoted. Even when we struggle, we can say with Paul that we do it "with all the energy Christ so powerfully works in me." (Colossians 1:29 NIV).

When I talk about movement in this book, this is what I mean: *a bold, grace-powered, intentional, active, and tenacious response to God's call on my life.*

Bold means having the courage to act or speak fearlessly despite real or imagined dangers. Boldness is not to be confused with brashness or aggressiveness that seeks to defeat others in an attempt to make things happen by mere force of will. The early believers prayed for boldness when facing opposition (Acts 4:29–31), and I believe we should pray for supernatural boldness too!

Grace-powered means we know that movement doesn't start with our strength, depend on our wisdom, or end with our glory. We partner with God and depend on him daily.

Intentional means we aren't careless, selfish, uncontrolled, or held captive by our own emotions or the responses of others. We respond to God's call with courage, conviction, and clear-headedness, and we are willing to cut things out of our lives that get in the way of fulfilling God's purposes.

Active means we aren't waiting around, looking for someone else to drag us along, or depending on past effort to maintain present momentum. We take the initiative and use our God-given gifts.

Tenacious means we don't quit when obstacles seem insurmountable because we know our God loves to move mountains for his people. We press forward with courage, perseverance, and grit, trusting that the One who called us is faithful and will fulfill the dreams he gave us.

We are made to move. Are you ready?

Questions for Reflection

1. When you think of the busyness level of your life right now, what words come to mind? Do those words indicate a healthy rhythm or an unhealthy one?

2. This chapter defines movement as "a bold, grace-powered, intentional, active, and tenacious response to God's call on my life." When you read that phrase, what word or words stand out most to you? How are they relevant to your situation right now?

3. What is one area in your life where you think God might be nudging you to move?

Chapter 2

IT'S YOUR CHOICE

f God had tasked me with writing the Bible, I would probably have done things differently. Specifically, I would have included a lot more explanations. I love systems, diagrams, analysis, lists, and well-reasoned arguments. A good Venn diagram? Poetry. A five-year church growth plan? Now you're speaking my language.

God did not ask my opinion, however. And instead of reams of information and analysis, God chose to reveal himself largely through a genre I'd have probably forgotten about: stories. Stories (technically, the genre is called "narrative") comprise 44 percent of the Bible. Poetry is a distant second at 33 percent, and prose discourse (such as the New Testament letters) makes up only 23 percent.[2] Where I would have dedicated entire books to detailed systematic theology, God more often chose to reveal himself through the simple stories of people.

God knew what he was doing, of course. Stories have a unique power to engage our attention by stirring our emotions. We connect on an experiential level with the characters in each story. We feel their pain and share in their joy. And, when their lived experience resonates with ours, we learn from them.

That has been the case for me as I have studied the life of Abraham (known as Abram earlier in his life). I've preached on Abraham many times over nearly three decades of pulpit ministry. But as I moved into the senior pastor role at Mannahouse, our preaching team led our church through a study on Abraham's life as if it were the first time I had preached on his story. And Abraham's experiences resonated with me in a way I never expected.

Obviously, the specifics of Abraham's life and my own differ. I'm not a fan of deserts, living for years in a tent, going to war to rescue a wayward nephew, or having to wake up every day before the invention of coffee.

But the challenges he faced as a father and a leader, the pain of grief and loss he endured, and the grit he needed to move forward—those I understand. Probably no person in Scripture better illustrates the power of movement in response to God's call than Abraham. His life offers a fascinating model of both the blessings and the challenges of obeying the voice of God.

A Legacy of Quitting

Arguably, no human being in history has been revered by more people than Abraham. He was a respected patriarch and chieftain in his own time, but his legacy has spread far beyond mere local influence. Both Jews and Arabs trace their lineage to him, and he is esteemed to this day as a father of the faith by three of the world's most influential religions: Christianity, Judaism, and Islam.

But his life wasn't easy, and his response to God's call illustrates both the fruit of faith and the fallout of fear. His journey was messy and complicated, and from his perspective, it didn't always make sense at the time.

I don't know about you, but that sounds a lot like my life, too.

If you're familiar with the story of Abraham, you know that God called him to leave his home and travel to a new land, the land of Canaan, which God had promised to give to him and his descendants as their inheritance. What you may not know is that this road trip to Canaan didn't actually begin with Abraham. It started with his father, Terah.

It was Terah who had the original goal of reaching Canaan, according to Genesis 11:24–32. We don't know if God spoke to Terah directly or not, but something motivated him to gather his family together and leave his hometown of Ur for Canaan.

But Terah never made it. Before they left Ur, Terah's son Haran died. And if that wasn't painful enough, his son Abraham's wife, Sarai, was unable to have children—a tragedy and source of shame in that culture. We don't know much about Terah, but we know he moved toward Canaan and, as he journeyed, he experienced the grief and pain of loss. That may have been what motivated him to stop his journey once he arrived at the town of Haran. In English, the town's name is the same as that of his dead son. While there's a slight variation between the words in Hebrew, they would have been close enough that Terah may have been reminded once again of his lost son.

> Our words don't reflect the complexity of reality if we proclaim victory without the battle and joy unaccompanied by grief.

So, faced with the grief of loss and the challenges he knew still lay ahead, Terah quit. He gave up on his goal of reaching Canaan and settled instead in Haran. Stopping seemed easier in the moment than pursuing the dream in his heart.

Great pain can do that. Grief, disappointment, broken hearts, and shattered dreams—those types of hurts can make us want to just give up. Instead of forging ahead, we search for a place that minimizes the pain, and we find ourselves tempted to relinquish the dream that had once motivated us. As I read the story of his journey, I can almost hear him say, "I am Terah, the one whose son Haran died." Like him, we often become known by pain and loss. It's the place we live, and it becomes our very identity.

This tendency exists because we often live with a subtle expectation—so subtle that we often don't even realize we have it—that when we obediently respond to God's call, the immediate result will be pleasant. We assume that obeying God will feel good, that his path will be one of minimal resistance, and that any obstacles will conveniently melt away when we face them.

Those of us who pastor and preach can sometimes inadvertently contribute to this idea. We want to stir faith in our congregation and help people have hope, so we preach optimistic messages focused on God's power. But our words don't reflect the complexity of reality if we proclaim victory without the battle and joy unaccompanied by grief.

As my friend Ed Holmes once said, "It's not all puppies and unicorns." Sometimes, it's rainstorms and thorns. The book of Ecclesiastes puts it this way:

> There is a time for everything,
> and a season for every activity under the heavens...
> a time to weep and a time to laugh,
> a time to mourn and a time to dance...
> a time to search and a time to give up.
> (Ecclesiastes 3:1–6)

Grief, loss, resistance, acceptance of painful reality—these are facets of life on a broken earth. God is greater than any of those, and there is great joy in the journey. But movement isn't easy. And following God's call does not eliminate pain.

When Our World Shatters

On August 4, 2020, my family's world turned upside down. My wife, Michal, had called me midday when I was at the office to tell me I needed to take our twenty-one-year-old daughter Mariah to the doctor immediately. Michal isn't an alarmist: in twenty-one years of parenting, she had never spoken with this kind of urgency, even though our kids had all lived a very adventurous, risk-filled life. I dropped what I was doing and rushed home to find Mariah curled up under a blanket in a desperate attempt to block out all light. She'd had a severe migraine for a week, but the crescendo of pain had become unbearable. Something was seriously wrong.

What I didn't know is that in the days prior to this call, my wife had taken Mariah to the doctor twice and had done a video call another time. They had tried multiple prescriptions without success, and one had actually made the headache even worse.

We arrived at the clinic, and Mariah was taken to a dark room. After a brief exam, a very gracious doctor turned to me and said, "I can call an ambulance or you can take her to the ER to get a brain scan. Something is not right."

I took Mariah to the car in a wheelchair and then drove to the hospital. All the while, I was praying for a solution to a situation I hoped would be quickly resolved.

Upon arrival, the triage team checked her in and placed her in a dark, private hospital room. They gave her intense IV medications to bring relief, which helped somewhat. Then they took her for a CT brain scan while I waited. As a dad, every minute she was gone felt like an hour.

Three doctors came back into the room where we had been waiting just a few minutes later, wheeling a cart with a computer and a large screen on top. One doctor knelt by her bed in the dark room and said, "Mariah, would you describe this headache as the worst one you've ever had?"

"Yes," she murmured, exhausted by a week of agony.

His reply was simple, "There is a reason for that, and at least we know now."

He turned the cart around so we could see the screen, then he showed us the image they'd taken of my little girl's brain. I'll never forget what we saw: a large mass consumed the entire central portion of her brain. As I stared in disbelief, he said that Mariah was at imminent risk of a stroke and bleeding out and needed to be rushed to a different hospital for emergency surgery. Nurses flooded the room, starting IVs with steroids to relieve the swelling in an attempt to save her life.

In shock, I called Michal. We cried together as we made plans for her to meet us at the hospital. I texted my sister, who is a veteran nurse, as well as some of our closest friends. I couldn't even find words to pray, but my spirit began to pray with groans that came from the deepest places of my soul. I opened my music app and flipped through my library of songs. I stumbled upon Kari Jobe and Cody Carnes' song "Blessing," put it on repeat, and began to go back and forth between prayer in the Spirit and singing the words of the song.

When Michal arrived, the hospital staff initially refused to let her in. Due to the ongoing COVID-19 pandemic, family member access was restricted. We appealed, and the doctor finally intervened. "This is life and death," he said. "Let her in."

Mariah was rushed to another hospital by ambulance, where they put her in intensive care to see if they could get the situation under control. Thankfully the medications brought relief to the pain and swelling. The neurosurgeon wanted to do the surgery right away, but under the crushing weight of delayed surgical procedures due to the pandemic, he said it would probably be weeks or even months before space would open in their operating room schedule. Feeling like meds would keep her from hemorrhaging, they sent her home.

Just a couple days later, we received a surprise call from the neurosurgeon. He had gone home the same day Mariah left the hospital and said to himself, "Mariah's surgery cannot wait." He called in a special staff to perform surgery on a day where the operating room was technically supposed to be closed. That move on his part was a miracle moment we'll never forget.

When the day of surgery came, we had to check her in at the front desk, but COVID-19 restrictions didn't allow us to go on into the hospital with her. Mariah had trouble walking by this point and often did not know where or even who she was. Watching her wander into the hospital by herself was a horrible experience for us. My wife and I stood in front of the building and cried together.

About twenty minutes later, a nurse called my phone. She said that when Mariah got up to pre-op, she collapsed in her arms in tears. The nurse told us that if my wife and I would go to a side door, she'd sneak us into the pre-op area to be with our daughter. When we met her at the door, she said, "I recognized your name. You may not know me, but I go to your church. You should be with your daughter." I often think of her and thank God for her kindness to us.

After standing in the pre-op room and watching the staff wheel her towards the operating room, we cried and retreated to the court-yard outside the hospital. No one was allowed to stay in the hospital waiting room due to pandemic restrictions.

More than fifty of our friends and family showed up that day to sit on lawn chairs outside the hospital with us while we waited. After nearly six hours, the call finally came. The surgery had been deemed a success: the surgeon had been able to remove a large portion of the tumor, and Mariah made it through the process like a champ. They told us the tumor was most likely benign but that they had sent it off to be biopsied just to be sure.

It had been a traumatic few weeks, but we seemed to have dodged a bullet. Now, we could focus on recovery. We knew the road ahead would be tough, but things were going to get better. At least, that's what we thought.

But, we were wrong.

One month after her surgery, Mariah and I sat in her bedroom, talking with the neurosurgeon. We reeled in shock at the results of the biopsy. The tumor was malignant, with a high likelihood of grow-ing back in the brain and spine. This kind of tumor was so rare that they had done extensive consultations with three major cancer cen-ters across the nation, trying to figure out what it was and what to do. They had no answers. Their prognosis was that Mariah was unlikely to recover, even with chemotherapy and radiation.

We were devastated. After the doctor hung up, we drove to the wellness studio that Michal owns to break the news to her. Standing in that little room, the three of us wept and stared at one another in dis-belief. This wasn't supposed to happen. This couldn't be happening.

I can't explain the tsunami of emotions that engulfed me at that time. If you've been through something similar, you know already. If not, no words can really describe the pain, the horror, the anger, and the fear of hearing your daughter is probably going to die. I would do anything for my kids, and now my precious daughter, only twenty-one years old, was in a fight for her life—and I was helpless to protect her.

At that point, we had two choices to make. The first choice was external. We had to work through the various medical options, none of which were good or promising, and decide on a course of action. We opted for chemotherapy and radiation while also cutting out various types of food that could contribute to negative health outcomes.

The other choice we had before us was internal. How would we, as a family, respond to this? The temptation to be overwhelmed by grief, fear, anger, and bitterness was real.

Our family went away for a weekend, and we planned our next move together. We committed to fight—not only the cancer but also the fear. We had lived our lives in obedience to God's call, wherever that took us. And while we'd never faced a challenge like this one, we knew we needed to keep leaning into his character and promises. We weren't going to let fear, grief, or any other negative emotions cause us to give up on the dreams God had put in our hearts. We would not let this be our Haran.

> While we'd never faced a challenge like this one, we knew we needed to keep leaning into his character and promises.

During that family trip, I thought of several people who, like Terah of old, had really gone off the rails during a time of crisis. I read about Paul's warning to his son Timothy to hold fast to faith and a good conscience in order to keep from shipwreck. The Lord used those verses to establish a fixed point of reference in our lives that it was possible to be in a storm without being shipwrecked by suffering the loss of our faith, hope, or love.

We committed to moving forward.

That sounds noble as I write this. But in those next months, sometimes "moving forward" meant sobbing my heart out at 4 a.m. on the living room floor as I battled terror. Sometimes, it meant listening as my sons verbalized their anger, confusion, and pain at a God who would allow this to happen. Sometimes, it meant just surviving another day of appointments, tests, and the horrible side effects of chemotherapy.

In the coming months, other crises hit our family. My wife's business had to completely shift its schedule and strategy due to COVID-19 restrictions. My mom, who was a larger-than-life figure in our family, passed away. One of our sons had a severe medical emergency and was on life support for almost three days.

Today, miraculously, Mariah is still alive. She completed her Bachelor of Theology degree while navigating brain surgery, chemo, and radiation, earned her master's degree in Organizational Leadership from Regent University, and started a job at Portland Bible College. She is thriving in every way. The kind of cancer she was diagnosed with is so rare that the doctors pointed to thirty-five cases in the last ten years, of which 100 percent died, most within a year. Three years after the fact, she's breaking all records and the doctors stand amazed.

That doesn't mean our battle is over. She still has to get periodic scans and is on an experimental drug regimen that controls much of her life. Those familiar negative emotions still threaten to overwhelm us every time we have to go for a scan. Our son miraculously recovered. The doctors don't even know how he made it through. And my wife fought through the dark season of COVID-19 business closure and has rebounded from it. In all of these things, we haven't stopped moving forward, and we believe our family's best days are yet to come. God has been so good.

Life on a sin-broken planet hurts. You can't avoid all of the pain, and you can't control the tragedies that come your way. But God is offering you an opportunity:

To join him.
To leave where you are.
To break the inertia that is holding you back.

To move beyond the generational weight that would keep you in your own version of Haran.
To break decades of addiction and cycles of defeat.
To move toward promise despite pain and loss.

You don't have to quit when you hit a roadblock or suffer a loss. You don't have to let the pull of trauma cause you to untether from faith and a good conscience. You don't have to give up on the dreams God has placed in your heart. You can choose to move forward.

And when you do, the real adventure begins.

Questions for Reflection

1. Have you ever had an experience that made it feel difficult or even impossible to move on? What happened?

2. In times of pain or difficulty, have you seen God's graciousness, power, or purpose? How?

3. Are you facing any situations right now that make you tempted to quit? If so, how could you lean into God's grace in order to move forward?

Chapter 3

A DESERT AND A DREAM

H aran was the end of Terah's story, but it wasn't the end of God's story. God still had a plan for the family, a plan that would affect all of history. And he chose Abraham to set the next stage of that plan into motion. Genesis records God's call:

> The Lord had said to Abram, "Go from your country, your people and your father's household to the land I will show you.
> "I will make you into a great nation,
>   and I will bless you;
> I will make your name great,
>   and you will be a blessing.
> I will bless those who bless you,
>   and whoever curses you I will curse;
> and all peoples on earth
>   will be blessed through you."
> (Genesis 12:1–3)

When I read that, it's easy for me to imagine Abraham responding with eagerness and faith. What an amazing promise! Who wouldn't want to be blessed, become famous, be protected by God himself, and someday be a blessing to literally every nation on earth?

But read it again. Notice what this promise is missing? A strategy! There is no business plan. There is no means of financing this endeavor. There isn't even an actual geographic goal stated in the text.

God didn't give Abraham any details whatsoever—just a big challenge and an even bigger promise. It's easy for us, looking back at the whole story from our perspective now, to assume that it was a no-brainer for Abraham to leave Haran and set out for the land God was promising him. But it wasn't that simple.

Imagine being Abraham. You're sitting comfortably in Haran, surrounded by family, servants, and possessions. Your business is doing well, you're respected, and you enjoy the company of your father's house. Then, one day, a voice out of nowhere tells you to leave all this. That voice says to pack up your family and head into the desert in search of a mystical land where you'll be blessed beyond your wildest dreams. Wouldn't you wonder if the dates you were snacking on might have been a little fermented?

As far as we know, Abraham wasn't living in sin or failure before God called him. In fact, God had blessed him greatly. Abraham had accumulated wealth and power during his time in Haran (see verse 5).

This is an important point for us to understand. Just because we are experiencing success in our lives doesn't mean we have arrived at God's end goal for us. God can bless us for a while in one place, then challenge us to leave behind the stability of that place to step into something new he is preparing for us. God's calling isn't always to bring us out of disobedience—often, it's to move us from the place where he's blessed us into a place where we can be a blessing.

Abraham had already experienced God's blessing, but nothing like what God had in store for him next. God's words gave Abraham a dream worth risking everything for. But the dream wouldn't come without a cost. But the dream couldn't come true without movement. There was a desert to cross, after all.

God's Calling Is Costly

Abraham gave up the financial stability of Haran. He left behind the respect and influence his wealth and family connections had given him in the community. He said goodbye to his fathers household.

He started over, risking everything to see the fulfillment of his God-given dream.

It's no different for us. While we may not have to leave everything we know and learn how to live in a literal desert, obeying God's call will often cost, at least in the short term.

I remember the first time I really felt the cost of obeying God. I'm a city pastor now, but I grew up in rural farmland on an island (yes, an actual island) in the middle of the Columbia River in the Pacific Northwest part of the United States. As a teenager, my family raised cows for beef and I owned several animals of my own. I bought them with money that I earned by working for local farmers and business owners, and I cared for and loved them deeply. My favorite animal was a black Morgan horse named Aslan. If you're a horse lover, you understand the bond that develops between a person and a horse. It's unique, indescribable, and priceless.

> Obeying God's call will often cost, at least in the short term.

After I graduated from high school, I felt God calling me to Portland Bible College. I knew I was hearing his voice. I knew he had created me to pastor others and that this was the training I needed. But to cover the tuition, I would have to sell my beloved horse.

Making the decision was hard, but following through was even harder. Although I knew it was the right thing to do, nothing had ever hurt so badly before. As I stood in my driveway, watching the horse trailer drive away with my prized horse, I wept. I gave up the thing in life that was dearest to me, and I did it because the Lord asked me to. Obeying God that day meant walking a road of grief, sacrifice, and pain that I've never forgotten.

Decades later, I am so glad I went all in when God spoke to me. I benefit every day from the training I received in Bible college, and I can look back and clearly see how every step I took was sovereignly directed. The relationships I built and the place God directed me to go would become the very place God would call me to lead twenty-seven years later. The pain was real, but the dream was worth it.

Jesus didn't tiptoe around the cost of following him. At one point in his ministry, he had become so popular that huge crowds were showing up to hear him speak. Church-growth consultants would have told him to make discipleship as easy as possible to attract more people. But Jesus did the exact opposite. He told them that following him would mean picking up their own cross. It would mean rejection by family members. He capped it off with, "So then, none of you can be My disciple who does not give up all his own possessions" (Luke 14:33 NASB). You can imagine how that went over with his listeners!

Of course, Jesus wasn't demanding that every follower literally sell all their possessions. But they needed to be willing to if that was what it took to obey the call! Jesus wants us to give up our dependence on material things, our obsession with accumulating more, and even our control of what he's given us already.

When he asks us to move, the cost is real. But God's call is always worth the price we pay.

Who's in Control?

The tangible things we sometimes need to give up in order to obey God—our money, some free time, a hobby, or a vice—are costly. But there is a greater and more subtle price we must pay. It's not the things themselves that are so important, after all. It's what they represent to us: stability, predictability, status, and safety.

Very often, the hardest thing to give up is the loss of control. Or, more accurately, it's the loss of the illusion of control.

We love stability and predictability. It feels safe, and there's nothing wrong with that. It's smart to analyze risks, avoid unnecessary danger, and make wise decisions. "Count the cost before building the tower" is a word of guidance and wisdom before embarking on any faith journey with the Lord. But too often, our desire to be stable is born out of a stealthy fear that we won't be safe unless we are in charge. We say we trust God—and we even think that we do—but our need for control reveals a somewhat more complex reality.

Abraham certainly felt that tension. He was trading out a life of stability and predictability in Haran for the uncertainty of nomadic life in a hostile desert. He knew what it meant to risk everything to obey God's call.

When God asks us to move, and when that move means risk, we find out how much we trust him. That's a humbling experience because, more often than not, our level of trust is less than we thought it was.

Fortunately, God isn't fazed by that. He works with us, for us, and through us despite our weaknesses. He gives us the ability to say yes to his call and then helps us follow through. Philippians 2:13 says, "For it is God who works in you to will and to act in order to fulfill his good purpose."

God doesn't override our free will. We actually get to choose, and our choices matter. But he is there every step of the way on our journey. And if our heart's desire is to obey God, he is faithful to help us do it.

We don't have to be in control of our lives. We really never were, to be honest. Yes, we can control some things and influence many others. But thinking that our efforts will guarantee success or always keep us from tragedy is just plain wrong. As the writer of Ecclesiastes says:

> The race is not to the swift
> or the battle to the strong,
> nor does food come to the wise
> or wealth to the brilliant
> or favor to the learned;
> but time and chance happen to them all.
> (Ecclesiastes 9:11)

I'm not at all suggesting we adopt some sort of fatalistic approach to life. The Bible is clear that our actions affect us and others. The creation account reveals that human beings, made in the image of God, are meant to function as co-regents with our Heavenly Father, ruling and reigning in this life. But I am suggesting that we give up the arrogant assumption that taking dominion, according to creative intent, means that we can guarantee the outcomes we desire (or even that those outcomes are the right ones anyway). Let's let God be God. He's really good at it.

God didn't ask Abraham to be perfect before he blessed him. God just asked him to obey. And thousands of years later, God hasn't changed a bit. He's asking you and me to obey. To surrender control of our lives. To move in response to his call. To trust him enough to risk. To pass through the desert and watch God fulfill his word and turn crazy dreams into reality.

The God of the Not Yet

One of the most amazing descriptions of God in the Bible is found in Romans 4. Paul, the writer of Romans, has been talking about the faith of Abraham and how we are Abraham's children because of our shared faith in God. In the middle of his argument, he drops this gem of a description of God: "[Abraham] is our father in the sight of God, in whom he believed—*the God who gives life to the dead and calls into being things that were not*" (verse 17, emphasis added).

God gives life to what is dead and calls into reality things that don't yet exist. He did it for Abraham, he's done it for me, and he'll do it for you.

Is there something God put in your heart that has died? Is there a dream you have given up on? A not-yet-reality that you have decided was just a fantasy? An idea too big and bold and risky for you to believe it could ever happen?

If so, I have some news for you: God hasn't changed. He's still in the business of bringing the dead to life. He still loves to make something out of nothing. He's a restorer of broken hearts, a renewer of broken spirits, and a rebuilder of broken dreams.

I believe God is calling his people all over the world to move in response to his voice. I believe there are creators, innovators, businesspeople, pastors, missionaries, leaders, and influencers about to be unleashed on a world that desperately needs what you have to offer.

You may believe the negative words others have spoken over you or you have spoken over yourself. You may think you are incapable, disqualified, untrained, or unworthy. And you may be right! But that has never stopped God. He's the God who calls things into existence that don't yet exist. He's the God who takes imperfect people and uses them for his glory while he blesses, heals, and sanctifies them in the process. He has a plan for you, and it's bigger than you think.

That plan isn't just about improving your life or your relationship with him, although he'll do that too. God is calling you and me to something much, much bigger. He's asking us to join a global movement of his people that will impact every nation in the world.

Your life has meaning. You were created for a reason. And no matter what life, others, or the devil himself has thrown at you, God's purposes will prevail if you are willing to believe. He is calling you and waiting for your response.

All you have to do is move.

Questions for Reflection _____

1. Can you think of a time when you felt God was challenging you to take a step and move forward without telling you all the details? How did you feel? How did you respond?

2. Have you ever had to give up something valuable to you, whether tangible or intangible, in obedience to God? Looking back at that now, how do you feel about your decision?

3. Is there a dream in your heart (or a memory of a dream you once had) that seems like an impossible one? Is there a possibility God still wants that dream to come to pass? Why or why not?

Chapter 4

UP, IN, AND OUT

W hen we think of movement, we typically think of going someplace. But that's not the only kind of movement. In reality, the most important moves we make are usually not geographical at all. They are relational. If we are going to find our place in Jesus' movement, where every part of our lives breathes divine purpose, we have to start and end with relationships.

Relationships are a fundamental part of being human. God himself is relational. Before the creation of the world, he was the Triune God, existing in relationship as one God in three persons.

When he created humans, he didn't do so in order to have slaves who would do his dirty work for him, as other creation myths in ancient civilizations supposed. God created us because he wanted a relationship with us. This doesn't mean (as some theologians have thought) that God was lonely and created humanity to fill some sort of emotional need. The truth is that God needs nothing. God created us to further the scope of what already existed in the godhead—perfect, shared, harmonious, unified relationship.

He walked with Adam and Eve in the Garden of Eden, enjoying the beauty of sharing companionship with them. When they sinned and broke that relationship, When they sinned and broke that relationship, God's love for them motivated him to set in motion a plan to restore it that would cost him the life of his one and only son.

I encourage you to recognize and respond to God's voice when he calls you to move so that you can live the full life he has for you. He isn't looking for an employee or robot to carry out his instructions or do his work for him. Nor is he looking for a relationship to meet his own needs. He wants a relationship through which he can lavish his love on all who choose to receive it. All obedience and all God's blessings flow from a relationship with him.

Of course our actions matter. We are commanded to be holy (1 Peter 1:15-16). We were created to do good works (Ephesians 2:10) that glorify God. And we play a key part in his plan of redemption for this broken world! (We'll look at that in more detail later.) But all of that flows from our relationship with God and our relationships with one another. And since healthy relationships are never static, they will always involve movement.

There are three primary avenues of relationship, and I want to examine how the idea of movement relates to each. Chances are, some of these will come easier to you than others will. But while some might take more intentionality or effort, all of them are vital for you to become who God has created you to be. Believe me, it is worth the effort!

Up

Our first and most important relationship is upward, **closer to God**.

One day when religious leaders were attempting to trap Jesus with his words, they asked what the most important commandment in the law of Moses was. Jesus' reply not only stated a summary of the whole law, thus astounding the hearers, but it also emphasized our first step to break inertia in life and begin to move.

> "Jesus replied, 'You must love the Lord your God with all your heart, all your soul, and all your mind.' This is the first and greatest commandment." (Matthew 22:37-38 NLT)

If we have a healthy, growing relationship with God, every aspect of our life benefits. But if our relationship with him is broken, stagnant, or weak, every area of our life suffers as a result.

Jesus compared our relationship to him to that of a vine and its branches. If we stay connected to the vine, abiding in him, we grow and bear fruit. If our connection to the vine is broken, we begin to shrivel.

So how do we develop and maintain a healthy relationship with God?

We aren't chasing God. If anything, he's chasing us.

Before I suggest some practical ways to do that, I want to point out something that I think is maybe the most beautiful truth in all of Scripture. It's simply this: God *wants* to have a relationship with us. He values it more than we can possibly comprehend. He loved us enough to create us out of nothing and make us bearers of his image. He loved us enough to rescue us from our sin and selfishness. He loved us enough to watch humanity betray him and then send his own Son to die for us in response. He loves us enough to respond with compassion when we cry, patience when we fail, reassurance when we are weak, and faithfulness when we stumble.

We aren't chasing God. If anything, he's chasing us.

This is so encouraging to me. But if I'm being totally honest, it's also the hardest truth for me to embrace. I fall into the camp of those who struggle to believe that God loves me unconditionally. I wrestle with this tension every day, wishing I could just accept the truth of what I preach and what others tell me. Even as I write this, I'm aware that I have yet to fully experience the reality of this truth in my own life or the freedom that revelation brings.

In this struggle, when I feel far from God, am confused, feel ashamed, or am just plain weary, I have learned to confront my unbelieving heart and mind with truth. I reassure myself with the truth of God's Word. I remind myself that God chose me before I ever chose him. My responsibility isn't to convince some aloof deity to give me what I want by saying the right words or doing the right actions. It's to move toward a loving Father whose open arms are ready to embrace me. It's simply to respond to his love for me. I resist the gravitational pull that causes me to be stuck and spin my wheels, like the tractor in the mud when I was working by my house.

That work does involve faith and diligent obedience! And as we saw in Abraham's life, obedience can be both risky and costly. But our obedience is in response to God's choosing and call rather than a willful, works-filled attempt to earn his favor, and it is a loving response to the love of God that is driven by a relationship, not demanded by duty.

In that context, knowing that God has chosen us and loves us, how do we grow in our relationship with him?

As in any relationship, there are no magic formulas or shortcuts for our relationship with God. But I want to suggest three ways to respond to God that will help you move closer to him, regardless of where you're at now.

1. Respond with intentionality.

King David wrote, "When You said, 'Seek my face,' my heart said to you, 'Your face, LORD, I will seek'" (Psalm 27:8, NKJV). When you feel a desire in your heart to know God more, to hear his voice, or to obey something he's calling you toward, then obey! It's not complicated. When we obey God, moving intentionally in response to his call, we learn to hear his voice even better. We grow closer to him as we move toward him.

2. Respond with your time.

No relationship grows without an investment of time. Set aside time every day to be with Jesus. Early morning works well for a lot of people, but others prefer the evening, during their lunch break, or short times throughout the day. The key is to block out a set time when you won't be distracted and can focus on God. The more time you spend with Jesus, the more you become like him. (This simple concept is so important we'll spend an entire chapter looking at what it means.)

3. Respond with trust.

Sometimes God will show you the end goal and ask you to trust him to lead you there. Sometimes he will just show you the next step and leave the future shrouded in darkness for a while. Sometimes he'll give you both the end goal and the next step to take, but one or both of those will seem utterly impossible. Get used to that! God wants you to learn to trust him implicitly. He's patient when you doubt, and he won't give up on you just because you struggle to trust. But he is faithful to keep gently (and sometimes not so gently) putting you in places where you will learn the secret of trust in him. And that secret is priceless.

In _____

The second category of relationships involves moving **closer to each other**: our family, faith community, and our friends.

These relationships are a significant part of our lives. They can be a source of precious strength and joy or they can cause immeasurable pain. Sometimes, they can be both.

Jesus established this priority for his disciples by telling the Pharisees that second to moving closer to God, we should move closer to each other.

> "A second is equally important: 'Love your neighbor as your-self.'" (Matthew 22:39 NLT)

Community is vital. We were not meant to live lonely lives. But it doesn't come naturally in many cases. One of the greatest weaknesses of Western post-industrial culture is its failure to foster true community. The Bible, however, was written in an ancient Eastern culture that deeply valued communal living, hospitality, community, and interconnectedness. We must be careful that we don't interpret the Bible through a Western mindset and filter, thus misunderstanding the message.

Dr. Vivek Murphy, the Surgeon General of the U.S., recently released an advisory aptly titled "Our Epidemic of Loneliness and Isolation." In it, he notes that 50% of Americans reported feeling lonely even before the COVID-19 pandemic cut millions of people off from their relational support networks. In addition to the emotional toll of loneliness and social isolation, the health risks are dramatic—the mortality impact of social isolation is equivalent to smoking up to fifteen cigarettes a day. It can raise the risk of premature death by 26 percent and increase the chances of heart disease, stroke, anxiety, depression, and dementia.[3] Loneliness, ironically, tends to be greatest in urban areas.[4] Surrounded by people, we are all alone.

So what do we do? How do we strengthen those relationships that are so central to our own well-being and to the health of those around us?

There is no shortage of information on the topic, that's for sure. There are countless videos, articles, books, and essays dedicated to the idea that you can have better relationships. Some of the advice is great, some is cliché, and some is honestly pretty terrible. But all of it points to the truth that we humans know we need one another.

I won't give you a list of quick life hacks to magically fix your relationships, because there are no shortcuts. As with anything truly valuable, you have to put in the work. But if you really want to strengthen your relationships—if you want to move *in* toward others—you will find that it's worth the effort.

Here are a few things that have helped me strengthen the relationships that mean the most to me. They aren't secrets. In fact, they are mostly common sense. But they work. If you want healthier, stronger relationships with those you love, ask yourself if God is nudging you to respond in one of these areas.

1. Learn to listen.

Communication is essential to relationships, but sometimes the best way to communicate is not to say anything at all. Relationships thrive only when two people truly care about one another, and nothing communicates caring more than being willing to listen. Brenda Ueland wrote, "Listening is a magnetic and strange thing, a creative force. You can see that when you think about how the friends that really listen to us are the ones we move toward... When we are listened to, it creates us, makes us unfold and expand."[5]

Marriage therapists recognize the power of listening in bringing healing to hurt relationships. They will lead clients through simple listening exercises such as the Gottman-Rapaport Intervention[6] that are designed to help one spouse honestly share their own feelings while the other practices truly listening. It's harder than it sounds, and it's more powerful than you'd ever imagine. Often, major areas of tension and conflict can move toward significant resolution simply by taking time to listen with openness and empathy.

If you want to grow a relationship, try moving toward the other person by actively taking a posture of listening.

2. Schedule the chaos.

Relationships are messy, unpredictable, and time-consuming. This is especially the case with family. We raised three kids. None of them ever wanted to talk about deep, meaningful things when it was convenient for me. If I said, "How was your day" or "How are you really doing?" I'd usually get a very basic response (or just a grunt). But at midnight, when my brain cells had mostly gone to sleep and my body was ready to follow, one of them would decide they wanted to talk. Or it might happen when I was behind on a deadline, or heading to a meeting, or just in kind of a bad mood myself. But I would drop what I was doing, summon all my attention, and engage with them when they were ready to open up to me. Those unplanned moments were priceless, life-changing encounters.

The fact is, relationships don't submit to calendars. They weren't meant to. Their messiness doesn't fit into our time-conscious, agenda-driven world. So, here's a thought: schedule in some time for the inevitable chaos of a people-filled life. Instead of cramming every single minute of your day full, deliberately leave some time free. If that gets filled up with a crisis, then congratulations—you planned ahead, so resolving that crisis won't inadvertently cause another. If no crisis occurs, take a nap!

Since you can't add more hours to your day, this means you will likely have to remove a few things from your current schedule. That may feel impossible. It certainly does for me. But if a big enough crisis occurs, those things are going to get dropped anyway. Some things that feel essential are actually not as vital as we think. My daughter's cancer upended all our lives and taught us that many of the things that fill our calendars and to-do lists are not as important as we think they are—and how meaningful some "little" things really are. Sometimes when I get sucked into the vortex of ministry and family responsibilities, it's helpful to stop and look at my schedule through the lens that cancer gave us. In the face of life and death, what actually matters? I want to be sure I don't miss those things because of the busyness of life.

Moving toward others means leaving space—both time and energy—for people to be unpredictable. As you plan your day and your week, learn to consciously build in some buffer time so that you can be fully present when the need arises. Your relationships will grow as a result.

3. Be willing to set healthy boundaries—and respect those of others.

"Boundaries" has become a buzzword in the last few years, and for good reason. Sometimes, the most loving thing we can do is to say no. True love is willing to sacrifice for the other person, but it doesn't ignore another person's abuse, take responsibility for that person's failures, or rescue them from the consequences of their actions so that they can continue to act in unhealthy ways. Love never means giving up our own agency in a situation.

Love doesn't mean expecting others to do that for us either. Sometimes we look to other people to rescue us from our negative feelings or to enable us to continue in a lifestyle that isn't actually healthy. Instead of turning to God for comfort and obeying him when he points out something in our lives that needs to change, we cling to others and expect them to do God's job—or ours—for us. When we lean too heavily on people around us, we pressure them to violate God-given boundaries of their own.

One of the best books I've read on this topic is *Boundaries*, by John Townsend and Henry Cloud. I highly recommend it as a means to help develop relationships that are healthy and mutually beneficial. If the issue of boundaries continually sabotages your relationships, consider also meeting with a Christian therapist or a trusted mentor who can help you understand what is motivating you to act the way you do and how to grow in this area.

4. Embrace the essentiality of church

When it comes to communities, I can think of no place more powerful, life-giving, and growth-producing than a healthy local church. The local church is God's primary instrument to advance his movement. It is—or is meant to be—a community of believers who share in each other's lives, supporting each other in times of trouble and rejoicing with each other in times of triumph. It is where unconditional love meets mutual accountability.

If you attend our church, you hear the concept of community celebrated regularly. We love one another and believe that shared life is central to the gospel. We aren't perfect! Every one of us is a work in progress. But we are committed to one another and to the movement we are a part of. We love, forgive, confront, support, listen, strengthen, and celebrate one another.

As a pastor, I know more about the complexities of church communities than most people. Like you, I've experienced both the good and the bad. I've been loved, cared for, blessed, and supported. I've been hurt, ignored, and slandered. I've been tempted to lash out at others, and, truthfully, I have been tempted to just leave the church altogether.

But despite the complexities and the imperfections inherent in any relationship, I'm committed to staying the course because I believe the church is the bride of Christ (Ephesians 5). Jesus loves every local church because each is a part of his beloved bride, and he is committed to helping us make those communities reflections of his character, heart, purpose, and family.

In times of crisis in my personal life or the life of our family, members of our church have carried our burdens with us. They have reached out with love, grace, understanding, wisdom, and practical help. And I'm not the only one. Because of my role in the church, I hear about a lot of problems in people's lives, and time and again I have seen others come gladly to their aid. God did not create any of us to do life alone.

If you're not in crisis, it can be easy to think you don't need the church. I'd argue, though, that you need community more than ever. You need like-minded people who will encourage you to keep making wise decisions. You need to be challenged by God's Word, both preached from the pulpit and shared one-on-one by other members of the body. You need to develop relationships with people from other cultures, seasons of life, social circles, and age groups. You need to use your own gifts to bless others. You need the impartation and formation that come through all five "governmental gifts" in Ephesians 4. And you need to worship God in a gathering larger than your home to remind you of God's greatness and your placement among his people. All of this happens in the context of a local church community.

Church isn't primarily a religious service. It's a community. And it's one of God's greatest gifts to you if you will invest the time and energy to become part of it.

Out

The third category of relationships is the one we could often think the least about, but it is at the core of fulfilling God's calling on our lives. He wants us to move not only *up*, closer to him, and *in*, closer to each other, but also *out*, **closer to the world around us.**

When you observe and reflect on Jesus' first act after forty days of fasting in the wilderness, you can learn a lot about his movement. Rather than renting a colosseum or launching a marketing campaign, he called two disciples to follow him. I've meditated on that verse for countless hours over the last few years, and I've come to believe it contains the seed of Jesus' movement.

"Jesus called out to them, 'Come, follow me, and I will show you how to fish for people!'" (Matthew 4:19, NLT)

> Jesus called them UP—closer to God
> Jesus called them IN—closer to each other
> Jesus sent them OUT—closer to the world around them

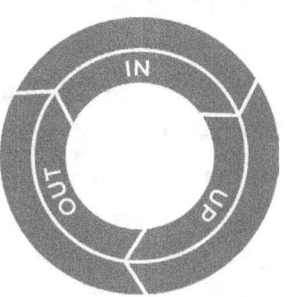

We interact with people outside of our faith community every day. Co-workers, members of organizations we belong to, strangers in the grocery store, and neighbors—we constantly rub shoulders with people.

These are people God loves. People who are hurting. People who need what you and I have to give. People who need to be served and loved and accepted.

People who are easy to ignore.

Too often, we are so focused on meeting our own needs or achieving our own goals that our interactions with others are limited primarily to what they can do for us or what they might take from us.

When we are driven by selfishness, ambition, or fear, we stop seeing people as people. They become forces to control or problems to avoid.

But when our relationship with God is intact and we are able to fully depend on him to meet our needs and to keep us safe, we are free to move outward, toward the world around us. It's a world full of people he loves. After all, Jesus died for the server who brought your food the last time you ate out, the homeless person clutching a cardboard sign that you pass every day driving to work, the couple who has a different view on marriage, and the neighbor whose political stance is the polar opposite of yours.

My wife and I had a unique experience early in our ministry journey that codified this into our ministry philosophy. We had been married a little over a year and had just planted a church in a mid-sized community in Washington state (another key moment in my life where God's call meant surrendering everything to join his movement). A couple of times a week, we'd stop by a store down the street from our house to grab something we needed to complete our dinner preparations. A young man often waited on us, and we'd politely exchange greetings each time.

One evening, he said, "Hey, I've watched you guys, and I want to get to know you. I'm hoping to get married, and I'd like to build my life like you guys do." That started a relationship that led to him coming to our house for dinner, attending church gatherings, and eventually hearing the hope we had in Christ. That encounter showed us how important it was to live in, engage with, and move toward the world around us. There are people in need everywhere around us. Do we really see them? Are we willing to open our lives to them?

We are called to love people and to serve them. In the next section of this book, we'll explore this in greater detail because it's so vital. God's call on our life isn't just to know him more, and it isn't just to love our families more. He created us to make a difference in the world around us. Every aspect of our lives is drenched in divine purpose, but we must be willing to see it and respond.

Questions for Reflection _____

1. If you were to describe your current relationship to God (your "Up") in three words, what would they be? If you were to pick three words you wish described that relationship, what would they be?

2. Who makes up your community (your "In")? What relationships are strong and healthy, and which ones need some healing?

3. When you think about the world around you (your "Out"), what names or faces come to mind? Take a minute now to pray for them. Ask God if there is anything in particular you could do for one or more of them today. What do you feel he is saying?

A MODEL OF MOVEMENT

"Come, follow me," Jesus said,
"and I will send you out to fish for people."
Matthew 4:19

Chapter 5

HIGH INVITATION, HIGH CHALLENGE

During Jesus' life, he ministered to thousands (likely tens of thousands) of people. He told stories that made the crowds snicker and the religious authorities fume. He performed miracles of healing and provision. He treated the social outcasts and the sinners as real people worthy of being loved. He took time to bless little children and listen to the pain of broken people. Jesus was accessible, loving, and kind. He met people where they were.

But he didn't leave them there.

Jesus was a master of getting people to move. He didn't do it coercively, through manipulation or shame, nor did he demand they move through external control. He did it through invitation, grounded in relationship. He accepted and loved people unconditionally in a way that gave them motivation and hope. Then he invited them to embrace the radical changes they knew they needed to make.

But while he spent many hours teaching and healing the crowds, the ones he worked with the most were his disciples. Out of all the crowds who heard him preach and the curious throngs who followed him, Jesus chose twelve to be his disciples.

He focused his efforts on the disciples in a way he didn't do with anyone else. Jesus preached to the crowds, but he lived with the disciples. He healed the multitudes, but he mentored the twelve. He blessed the people who listened to him, but he washed the feet of his friends.

The Bible records the exact words Jesus used when calling the first two of these twelve:

> As Jesus was walking beside the Sea of Galilee, he saw two brothers, Simon called Peter and his brother Andrew. They were casting a net into the lake, for they were fishermen. "Come, follow me," Jesus said, "and I will send you out to fish for people." At once they left their nets and followed him. (Matthew 4:18–20).

We don't have a record of the words Jesus used to call the other disciples, but I imagine they were similar to this. Notice that this call included two key components: an invitation and a challenge. The invitation was that they would become fishers of men. The challenge was to follow him—literally.

Interestingly, this parallels Abraham's call, which also involved an invitation (to be blessed greatly) and a challenge (to leave his father's house and head out into the unknown). God's call always includes both invitation and challenge.

Jesus knew the world-changing message he brought, and he knew the best way to get that message to the world was through the transformational power of discipleship. So he invited a few people to walk with him, live with him, and be transformed by him.

He didn't just teach them theory. He demonstrated through his example, coached them in their weaknesses, gave them opportunities to succeed and fail, called them out on their bad attitudes, and loved them through every messy part of their lives.

Make Disciples, Get the Church

Discipleship is still the model of movement for the gospel today. We often put a tremendous amount of focus on the most public aspects of

Christianity, such as church services and large events. But while corporate worship and preaching are vital parts of Christian community and growth, on their own, they are not the totality of discipleship. Jesus spent much of his time and energy mentoring a small group of followers because he knew the power of discipleship to spark a worldwide movement. As pastor and author Mike Breen puts it, "If you make disciples, you always get the church. But if you make a church, you rarely get disciples."

> True discipleship is both high invitation and high challenge.

As a pastor, I'm passionate about discipleship. I want to be a better disciple of Jesus myself, and I want the people in my church to be his disciples as well. I know that is the only way to fulfill what God created us for. It's the pathway to purpose and the key to peace and joy. We were created to move in response to God's call. We were created to be his disciples.[7]

Discipleship is more than hearing good teaching and preaching. It's more than listening to Jesus' words or even receiving the blessings he offers us when we become part of his family. Discipleship is when we become committed to being more like Jesus ourselves and we dedicate ourselves to his purposes.

True discipleship is both high invitation and high challenge. Invitation refers to *the relationship that is inherent in discipleship*. We are invited to know Jesus as a friend and to become part of a grace-filled community where we can be safe even when we are hurting and vulnerable. Relationship, rooted in hospitality, is at the core of true discipleship.

But discipleship doesn't stop with being accepted into a loving community. It is also high challenge. When we accept Jesus' invitation to new life with him, we also accept his challenge *to become more like him and to share in his mission*. Jesus didn't just ask his disciples to listen to his sermons. He challenged them to pick up their crosses and follow him.

Jesus invited his followers into a movement that would transform both their lives and the world around them. It was a grace-driven, life-altering invitation to enter into a relationship with him and participate in, and yes, even advance his movement. And it was simultaneously a challenge to obey him even to the point of laying down their very lives.

High Invitation, High Challenge

The diagram below, based on material developed by Mike Breen and the Discipling Culture Collective, has helped me understand this concept better. It's been a useful tool for our church as we think carefully about who we are and what we want to focus on. And I believe it can help you to discern whether you are engaging in true discipleship or not.

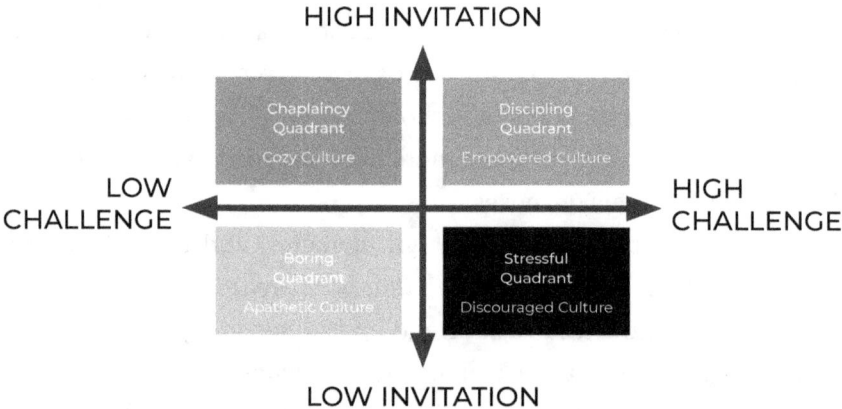

High invitation, low challenge.

If a culture, program, or cause is high invitation and low challenge (upper-left quadrant above), then it produces a cozy culture. It can be tempting for churches to build programs like this. After all, everyone likes to be comfortable. But while cozy is great for a vacation cabin in the woods, it's not the life we were built for. Yes, we can retreat into self-centered, comfort-focused living, but that's not discipleship.

Low invitation, low challenge.

If a culture or cause is low invitation, low challenge (bottom-left quadrant), then it's boring. It doesn't attract people, and it doesn't keep anyone's attention for long. People quickly grow apathetic and disinterested. I don't know about you, but I've been part of more than a few activities that fell into this quadrant. I'm afraid I've even led a few.

Low invitation, high challenge.

This type of culture or cause often attracts highly motivated, sincere people. Something deep inside us yearns to respond to a leader who confidently challenges us to achieve something great. But if there is no genuine relationship—shared life, patience with each other's weaknesses, compassion toward others' needs, love that supersedes the objective—then people get discouraged and eventually burn out. Countless churches and movements have fallen into this trap. Consumed by a desire to do everything that needs to be done, they have forgotten to love the people doing it.

High invitation, high challenge.

True discipleship, as Jesus modeled it, offers unconditional love and acceptance (high invitation). But it maintains the uncompromising conviction that we are called to be like Jesus and share his love with others (high challenge). This type of culture is empowering. People's needs are met and their gifts are utilized to bless others.

When we commit ourselves to being Jesus' disciples, we move from passive recipients to active participants in his movement. We aren't just sinners saved by grace, like shipwreck survivors being rescued by a passing boat. We aren't just part of the crowd following Jesus to hear what he'll say next or sick people hoping he'll heal us so we can be happier while we keep pursuing our own goals. And we aren't even merely servants doing Jesus' bidding.

When we become disciples of Jesus—when we accept both his invitation and his challenge—we become something much more incredible than survivors, observers, or servants. We become his friends (John 15:5). There is work to do. And we are called to obey and to serve. But even in that calling, we don't just work *for* Jesus, we work *with* him. We share in his life and we share in his calling.

In the last chapter, we described the three types of essential relationships: in, up, and out. When we become Jesus' disciples, we engage in all three:

> Up: Disciples move closer to God.
> In: Disciples move closer to each other.
> Out: Disciples move closer to the world around them.

That's discipleship, and that's how Jesus sparked a movement that is still changing lives today. It's far more than a series of classes, or stages and lights, or powerful preaching—it's the framework of a lifetime journey.

Those relationships can be symbolized by three images: the cross, the table, and the towel. *The cross* (Up) describes our relationship with Christ. He gave his own life to redeem us and bring us into relationship with him, and he calls us today to share in his sacrificial, mission-driven movement to restore the lost to true life with him. *The table* (In) describes how we interact with fellow believers, our families, and others in our spheres of influence. We don't just live alongside people; we open our hearts and our homes to them. We live with intentional hospitality, modeling our lives on Jesus' continual willingness to share a meal and a moment with anyone willing to do so. *The towel* (Out) represents our willingness to serve our communities, our nations, and the world. Just as Jesus washed the feet of his disciples in order to model how they should orient their lives in relation to others, we also want to cultivate hearts willing to serve those in need.

The beautiful thing is that all three relationships (Up, In, and Out) and all three images (cross, table, and towel) continually interact and overlap. Our upward relationship with God includes the community of believers with whom we worship him. Our inward relationships with those we love not only encourage each of us in our relationship with God but also provide a natural place to invite outsiders in to experience Jesus. Our outward service toward the world is itself a form of worship and a means to cultivate true relationships both with those we love and strangers we have just met.

The cross, the table, the towel. All three are high invitation and high challenge. All three are essential to true discipleship. All three are part of God's call on your life. And all three form the basis for how we make disciples in the church where I serve.

The Real Key to Success

I teach a class at Portland Bible College, so I regularly interact with young people who genuinely want to obey God's call on their lives. But often, they aren't totally sure what that call is or how to accomplish it. It can seem overwhelming at times. I'm happy to listen to them and to help them think through practical aspects of vision, preparation, and strategy. I love all of that. I'm a dreamer and designer at heart.

But ultimately, it isn't design or strategy that matters the most. It's not talent, skill, or opportunity, either. While those things matter, the one thing that will dictate whether you become and do all that God has created for you is simply this: are you willing to be Jesus' disciple?

Are you willing to spend time with him, listening to his words until your heartbeat is synchronized with his? Are you willing to move in response to what he tells you, allowing him to change your thoughts and priorities so that you can be more like him? And are you willing to do the things he did: love people, serve the poor and needy, preach the truth, live a life that honors God, and lay down your life for the cause of Christ?

The twelve disciples Jesus chose were nothing special. In fact, they often acted more like bumbling clowns or spoiled children than heroes of the faith. Even at the Last Supper, Jesus' final meal with his disciples on the night he was arrested and sentenced to death, the disciples got into an argument about which of them was the greatest! If I knew I was going to die that evening, I'd be looking for a sentimental, intimate evening with my closest friends. I'd expect sympathy, heartfelt words of affirmation, and hopefully an escape plan. Instead, he got empty promises, an earful of bickering, and betrayal.

This rag-tag group wasn't the smartest, most well-resourced, or most mature. They failed spectacularly at a crucial time, running away when Jesus was arrested. But he didn't give up on them, and they responded to him with repentance and renewed commitment. When the Holy Spirit filled them, they began to preach with such boldness and power that the world would never be the same. They didn't have a strategy. But they had been with Jesus, and they were ready to respond to his call. They were so effective that within a short time, even their enemies complained that they'd "turned the world upside down" (Acts 17:6, ESV).

I don't know about you, but that's encouraging to me. If God could use such an unimpressive, often embarrassingly immature group of misfits, then he can use me. I don't have to have every strategy right. I don't have to possess all the skill or talent in the world. I just have to be Jesus' disciple. I can do that. And so can you.

Not only that, but we can also use the same principles to help others become disciples of Jesus. That's a core part of being Jesus' disciple, after all. When Jesus challenged Andrew and Simon to leave their fishing nets and follow him, the invitation was, "I will show you how to fish for people!" (Matthew 4:19, NIV). That invitation was to a lifetime journey of transformation and movement—closer to God, to each other, and to the world around us.

In the next few chapters, we'll look at what it means practically to be Jesus' disciple and how those principles can help us invite others to follow him too. Jesus isn't just calling us to move, after all. He's calling us to join a *movement*—a worldwide kingdom that is continually advancing as more and more people come to understand Jesus' love.

Are you ready?

Questions for Reflection

1. Look back at the invitation/challenge diagram at the beginning of this chapter. What quadrant best describes your life? What quadrant best describes your church? Are you satisfied, or would you like to see change in some areas?

2. Our Up/In/Out relationships are illustrated in the three symbols of the cross, the table, and the towel. What do the three symbols mean to you personally? How have you experienced them?

3. Is there any particular area where you know that God is both inviting and challenging you to grow? What steps can you take to respond to his invitation and accept his challenge?

Chapter 6

TIME WITH JESUS

I n these next three chapters, we're going to look at three simple
ideas that are foundational to becoming Jesus' disciples and
helping others do the same. They aren't complicated, mysteri-
ous, or difficult to understand. In fact, their very simplicity means
we easily overlook them. But just because they are simple to grasp
doesn't mean they are easy to do. They will challenge your selfish
desires, run counter to the habits you've developed, and stir up
spiritual opposition. And they will require perseverance to really
see their benefit.

All three come from the idea of relationship that we've already
developed. All three flow from Jesus' invitation to us. And all three
include an element of challenge, because they require us to move.

The first is simply this: we become like Jesus by spending time
with him.

That's it. I told you it wasn't complicated. You're probably thinking, "Yeah, I knew that already." So let me ask you this: how much time
do you spend with him?

If we really believed that sentence wholeheartedly, I suspect all
of us—myself most definitely included—would be far less likely to skip
our daily prayer time or lose focus during a worship service. We'd be
eager to pray, to spend time in God's Word, and to worship alone and
in community with others.

I'm not saying this to make you feel condemned. God is far
more patient with us than we often are with ourselves. But I am saying it to challenge you to become intentional about spending time
with Jesus.

This is not a legalistic rule that will somehow curry favor with God or a religious rite to impress others. It's simply the nature of relationships: we become more like those we spend time with.

I took piano lessons my freshman year in college from a highly skilled instructor named Alynne who was known for her boldness and humor. You always knew where you stood with Alynne and what she thought. She didn't limit her observations to your music skills either. One day as we sat down for our piano lesson, she offered up some sound advice to get rid of a friend who was pulling me down. I didn't ask for the input, but I needed it. I reflect on that day often as a pivotal conversation in my understanding about the power of relationships for good or for harm.

We see this in the lives of the first disciples of Jesus. After the Holy Spirit descended on the disciples, filling them with the presence and power of God, they began to preach boldly. The controversy this caused in the community got Peter and John arrested. When they were dragged before the high priest and other religious leaders and interrogated, they preached to their judges and accusers too—and accused them of murdering the Messiah! (Peter was never known for his tact.) The passage says, "When they saw the courage of Peter and John and realized that they were unschooled, ordinary men, they were astonished, and they took note that these men had been with Jesus" (Acts 4:13).

> Discipleship begins and ends with being in the loving and holy presence of Jesus.

The disciples had spent time with Jesus, and it showed. When we spend time with him, listening to him and responding to what he says, it shows in our lives too. The more time I spend with Jesus, the more I want to be like him. The more I come to love him. The more I sense his presence, hear his voice, and find my own values lining up with his. Discipleship begins and ends with being in the loving, holy presence of Jesus.

Discipleship means accepting Jesus' love for us, demonstrated on the cross as he gave his own life to bring us back into a relationship with the God we had rejected. And it means accepting his challenge to pick up our own cross and follow him.

So, what does this actually *mean*? How do we spend time with Jesus? He may be always present, but he's never visible. You can't just invite him over for a cup of coffee like you would a friend. (I guess you could, but you'd end up drinking all the coffee.) If you're like a lot of Christians, you already believe that spending time with Jesus is essential, but you struggle with how to actually do it in a way that feels meaningful.

I'd like to give you a few principles you can follow.

After each principle, I'll suggest a few creative ways you can incorporate that truth into your life. The principles are applicable to everyone, but the strategies will vary by individual or even by season of your life. You might find that one idea resonates with you while another doesn't seem the least appealing. That's alright. Think of the strategies as a menu of options, not a blueprint you have to follow.

But, just like at a restaurant, don't be afraid to try something new either. You might be surprised by the ways you encounter God when you step outside of your normal approach and try something creative.

My deep desire is that you and I both would continue to grow in genuine, loving relationship with God and spending time focusing on him might become one of life's greatest joys.

Principle #1: Prioritize time alone with Jesus.

Every one of us has more to do each day than we have hours in which to do it all. If we don't consciously choose to do what is most important, then the tyranny of the urgent will dictate how our lives are spent. But if the only way we are going to become like Jesus is to spend time with him, then that needs to be paramount for us.

The godless culture around us, our own selfish desires, and the devil himself don't take breaks. They try to influence our choices every single day. We need to deliberately carve out time to be in God's presence, seeing his perspective on what we are experiencing, and listening to his counsel. Nothing else will substitute.

I suspect we all know this to be true. We know that we should be spending more time talking with and listening to God, but we often struggle to make it happen. Here are a few ideas to think about. All of them have been used by believers for centuries to draw closer to Jesus.

Set aside time each morning before you start your day. This one is so common that it's almost become a rule for some people, as if God is only happy if we begin each day by talking to him. I'm pretty sure he's not that insecure, actually. There is no requirement to pray in the morning. But it does have a couple of big advantages: it's easier to do because no other projects have yet gotten in the way, and it helps us get our focus on God before we jump into the day's work. Personally, I would highly recommend setting aside at least a few minutes before you dive into the craziness that awaits you the rest of the day. Dr. Mark Jones, the prayer pastor at our church, often says, "Just get your carcass to a 'set place' at a 'set time.'" Mark's life was radically changed, breaking a decades-long cycle of depression and anxiety, by learning to spend time in the presence of the Lord. He has helped hundreds, if not thousands, do the same. His website bewithjesus.org could be a game-changer for you if this first point resonates with you.

Pray at night. For night owls, this may work a lot better than first thing in the morning. You're awake, you're energetic, and you have some time to think through your day and process it with God. Even if you're not a night owl, setting aside a fifteen-minute time to "debrief" with God can help you close out your day in a healthy way.

Set multiple short times throughout the day. This is common in some spiritual traditions and actually makes a lot of sense. Rather than spending an hour in the morning praying, break your prayer time up: fifteen minutes in the morning before you do anything else, fifteen minutes at lunch, fifteen minutes in the late afternoon, and fifteen minutes before bed.

Move. I don't know about you, but when I sit down to pray I sometimes end up resting in God's presence a little too literally. Activities such as walking (even if that's just pacing up and down in your living room), kneeling for a few minutes, or bowing down can actually improve your focus and communion with Jesus. Our minds and bodies are connected more closely than we realize. Use that to your advantage.

Get out into nature. For some people, a hike in the wilderness makes them feel closer to God than just about anything else in the world. There is something about being surrounded by the beauty, majesty, and expansiveness of nature that reminds us how great and how good our God really is.

Use your creative abilities to express yourself. Many people pour out their thoughts, desires, and even pain to God through painting, sculpture, or dance. Our God-given creative abilities can be a profound way of talking to God and hearing his voice. What do you love to do? Whether it's gardening, writing, singing, or dancing, find ways to worship God that break you out of tradition and let you experience him in a fresh way.

Pray with other people. Don't always pray alone. Make time during the week to pray together with a trusted friend, your partner, or a small group. Share prayer requests and then pray for each other during the week as well. This kind of prayer doesn't just bring you closer to God; it knits your heart together in friendships with others.

Principle #2: Center your focus on the Word of God.

Nothing helps us know God's heart better than hearing his Word. And while God does speak directly to our hearts through his Spirit, the Bible remains the authoritative center of our understanding of God and truth. Time and time again I have found reading God's Word to be the thing that cuts through my confusion, lifts my downcast heart, challenges a stubborn sin, or uncovers a blind spot I hadn't seen. It's life-changing.

You probably already believe this. You know that reading the Bible is important. You may even have a regular habit of reading. If so, wonderful! If not, I encourage you to start. There is nothing more powerful for transforming your thoughts, priorities, and emotions than the Word of God. There are many ways to do this.

> **Read through the Bible from start to finish.** This seems the most logical to new believers, as it's the way most books are read. And for many believers, it works well. Just be aware that you'll spend a lot of time in some of the larger books of the Bible, and some books are easier to understand and apply than others.

> **You can also read a small portion from several parts of the Bible each day.** This makes it easier to stay consistent in daily Bible reading even when you're working through a book of the Bible that may seem slightly less exciting than some of the others. Bible apps with reading plans can help make this technique simple and keep you from losing your place.

> **Incorporate devotionals into your Bible study time.** Sometimes another person's perspective on a Bible passage can open your eyes to new ways of understanding and applying a passage.

Memorize Scripture. Spend a day or two each week just memorizing a couple of verses. On the following days, review those verses quickly before you move on to your regular Bible reading. Over time, add to those verses until you have memorized an entire chapter. That may sound impossible, but it's not if you're patient. You will be amazed how many times a passage you've memorized will suddenly be directly applicable to a situation that comes up in your life weeks or even months later. Get the Word in you so that it's in your heart when you need it!

Principle #3: Obey what God says.

Often, we have to move in response to God's voice. His Word and his Spirit aren't there merely to inform us or comfort us but to help us change. James warned his readers, "Do not merely listen to the Word, and so deceive yourselves. Do what it says" (1:22). This passage points out that not only is it useless to spend time in God's presence if we don't respond to it, but it's actually harmful because we become self-deceived. We think we are doing well because we can quote Bible verses or argue theological points, but if we are not moving in response to God's voice, we are actually worse off than before. We think we are fine, so we refuse to consider that we might need to change.

Obedience is usually straightforward. God isn't vague or hard to understand. In our hearts, if we're honest, we know what we need to do differently. We may not know the outcome, and we may not know everything we need to do in the future, but we know the next step. If God is pointing to something in your life that needs to change, he is also ready and willing to help you obey. Take the step of faith to do it. Here are some things that can help:

Talk to your pastor or a trusted friend about your struggles. Let them help you better understand what is going on. The devil loves to sow confusion into our hearts because confused people tend to freeze instead of move. Godly leaders, mentors, and friends can often help us discern what God is saying and how to respond.

Journal. Writing our thoughts down often helps us clarify what we are thinking and feeling. Journal as you pray for wisdom, discernment, clarity, and strength, and write down what you hear God saying.

If you fall, get back up. God isn't about to give up on you, so don't let a failure stop you. Repent, get help from someone if you need to, and move forward again in obedience. Old habits and ways of thinking don't change easily, and it will be a fight in many cases for you to obey God. He has made you a warrior. So fight!

MOVE

In our church, we often recommend a method of prayer that incorporates all three of the principles above. It's a useful way to structure your prayer time so that you go beyond merely reading a passage or saying a quick prayer and instead learn to hear God's voice for yourself. It's called the MOVE method of prayer, and if you use it daily, I believe you will move closer to God and become more like him.

It looks like this:

M – Mark. Read a passage of Scripture and mark the words that stand out in your mind. Don't overthink it; just mark the words that catch your attention.

O – Observe. Explore the meaning of the passage in its context. Read it a couple of times. Read the section before and after if you need to get the context. Consult a commentary or other study aid if something doesn't make sense. Get a sense of what the author meant when they wrote the original passage so that you understand the passage correctly.

V – Visit. Have a conversation with the Lord about what you read. Does he have something to say to you about the words you marked or something else in the passage? Tell God how the passage made you feel, what it brings to mind, what you hope and fear. Then be still and let him speak to you. Journal what you hear.

E – Envision. How has your perspective changed as a result of reading God's Words and listening? Is there anything he is asking you to believe or to do? Is there anything you need to lay down? If so, what is he giving you in exchange? Write down anything that you feel God is saying to you and how you can respond.

Developing a relationship with God isn't quick, and it isn't always easy. Some days you will feel close to him, while others you may feel like your prayers are bouncing off the ceiling! (They aren't, but I know the feeling.) Always remember that God wants a relationship with you more than you could possibly imagine. You're not chasing a remote, aloof God. He initiated this relationship, and he is wholly committed to you. Whether you feel like you're close to him or struggling to connect, he is by your side all the time. He will never leave you or forsake you, and as you continue to seek his face, you will find a relationship with him that brings life, strength, and joy.

Questions for Reflection _____

1. Have you ever found yourself beginning to talk or act like some-
    one you have been spending time with? Was that a good or a bad
    thing? Is there something about Jesus you'd love to see reflected
    in your own life as you spend time with him?

2. What activities help you sense the presence of Jesus and hear
    his voice? Are there any creative or nontraditional ways, such as
    a nature walk or expressing yourself through arts or dance, that
    have been helpful?

3. Read John 14:4–5. (If you have time, read the entire section,
    which includes verses 1–17.) Then spend a few minutes using
    the MOVE technique taught in this chapter to interact with the
    passage. How did it go? Was it useful? Would you do anything
    differently next time?

Chapter 7

LIFE AT THE TABLE

S aturday mornings at the Corbin house as I was growing up were often filled with the smell of pancakes, bacon, fried potatoes and onions, and joyful conversation. My mom was a great cook, and she loved to share her food with others. We often had eight or ten guests, along with our family, seated at the breakfast table on Saturday mornings.

Those Saturday mornings were my favorite day of the week. I never knew who would be there. But I knew there would be good food, laughter, prayer, and a sense of community that is hard to describe. It taught me a lot about what those who follow Jesus should practice.

Our table was central to our house and community. Our neighbors, church family, nuclear family, and acquaintances from work all sat around our table at different times. It was a place for nurturing not only the body but also the soul and spirit.

It was where my dad, as a new believer, met with one of our church's leaders to learn more about what it meant to follow Jesus. Every week for months, they studied together at the table, sometimes well into the early hours of the morning. And what my dad learned there, he shared with others.

I remember once waking up in the middle of the night to the sound of crying coming from our dining room. I stumbled out of my bedroom and saw a young couple sitting at our table. They had fought with each other that evening and, not knowing what else to do, drove to my parents' house for help. Despite the late hour, they knocked loudly until my parents woke up. My mom and dad listened to their pleas for help and responded with an invitation to come in and sit at their table.

When I entered the room, they were listening to the young couple and sharing their own wisdom with them, helping set their fragile marriage on a course for healing and resurrection life.

In the last chapter, I gave you a simple key to becoming Jesus' disciple: spend time with him. As we do that, we become more like him. We accept his love shown on the cross, we take up our own symbolic cross, and we move forward into a life that glorifies God because we live and act like Jesus. Our *upward* relationship with God is a core aspect of becoming a disciple.

> It is more than a meal; it is an invitation to share in life together.

But discipleship doesn't stop there. It also extends *into* our relationships with family, friends, and others in our sphere of relationships. This is where the table becomes transformational.

Throughout history, sharing a meal together has meant far more than just the simple act of eating food. It has conveyed trust, intimacy, desire for a relationship, and a sense of responsibility for the wellbeing of others. It is more than a meal; it is an invitation to share in life together.

Jesus understood this. He ate with his disciples, mentoring them over countless meals (Luke 15). He wove imagery of meals, especially feasts, into many of his parables (Luke 15:11–32; Luke 14:16–24). He miraculously provided food for over five thousand people who had been listening to him teach (Luke 9:10-15). He invited himself over to a tax collector's house for a meal (Luke 19:1–10). In fact, one of the complaints his enemies made about him was that he ate with tax collectors and sinners (Luke 5:30).

It wasn't about the food, of course. It was about fellowship. Giving and receiving hospitality were central to Jesus' ministry because discipleship was. And discipleship only happens through relationships.

I don't think it's a coincidence that food played a role in Jesus' interactions with his disciples after his death and resurrection. Luke 24 describes two dejected disciples of Jesus, aware of his death but as yet oblivious of his resurrection, as they walked along the road to Emmaus. Jesus himself joined them on their journey, but they didn't realize who it was at first. It was only when they shared an evening meal together, and Jesus broke the bread and blessed it, that their eyes were opened and they realized he was their Savior. Shortly after that, Jesus appeared to his disciples, scaring the living daylights out of them. In fact, they were so sure he was a ghost that he asked for food and ate it in front of them to prove he was really a living person. Food and fellowship were so much a part of Jesus' ministry that it was in the act of eating together that they recognized him once again.

The early Church understood this well. In the first two centuries of the Church's existence, believers gathered regularly together for *agape* (love) feasts. At these meals, which crossed gender, economic, and social boundaries, they ate and worshiped together. Verlon Fosner pulls from numerous ancient sources to describe these events in the words of firsthand observers:

> "There is ample evidence of an average evening at one of these dinner church gatherings, a service order of sorts. By the time of Ignatius in 115 AD, the dinner church was setting a tone of thanksgiving and a joyful resound of glad and generous hearts praising God, unlike the gloom with which the later generations surrounded the Eucharist. The joy of the Lord was pervasive in these fellowship meals. Also during that time, the Roman historian Pliny wrote to Emperor Trajan in AD 98-117 that these Christians were in the habit of meeting on a certain fixed day, singing a hymn to Christ, binding themselves not to commit wicked deeds; after which they partook of food, of an ordinary and innocent sort. Pliny also reported that these first Christians were talkative, passionate, and sometimes quarrelsome as they met over evening meals to read Paul's letters. We get another glimpse of an average evening at a dinner church gathering in Tertullian's

> words from Apologies 39:16-19 which states, "Our dinner
> shows its idea in its name, Agape. Whatever the cost, with
> that refreshment we help the needy. Only so much is eaten
> to satisfy hunger. After water for the hands come the lights;
> and then each, from what he knows of the Holy Scriptures,
> or from his own heart, is called before the rest to prophesy.
> Prayer in like manner ends the banquet."[8]

Over time, this aspect of church life became deemphasized.
By the third century, asceticism and a belief among some that
the broken bread and cup shouldn't be shared with sinners (who
were often invited to agape feasts) led to a debate at the Council
of Laodicea that ended with the banning of agape feasts. Centuries
later, the Reformation reinvigorated the Church, but it didn't bring
back the focus on the table. Instead of relationships and life at the
table, the Reformation focused heavily on intellectual assent to doctrines. Churches became more about preaching than sharing lives.
Doctrinal truth took center stage with meals together left out of corporate worship.[9]

I believe that we need to recapture what we lost. I'm not suggesting that churches should provide a full meal each Sunday. (Although
I suspect it would be very popular!) But I do think the sacredness
of radically ordinary hospitality and the power of fellowship need to
become once again central to who we are as the community of the
redeemed.

A phrase you'll hear over and over again at our church is "Life at
the table." It's more than a tagline; it's a calling, a way of life, and the
culture we are building.

The concept of the table, both literal and symbolic, is central to
our vision of what church should be. Church is more than just a group
of believers who gather to worship and hear the Word on Sundays. It is
a community of people who care for one another, share our lives with
each other, and open our homes and hearts to those around us.

I Need You

Life at the table means a number of things to us. I believe these truths are essential to becoming like Jesus and joining his movement. After all, Jesus didn't tell his followers to attend a seminar. He broke bread with them.

The first thing that means to us is one I've talked about already, but that bears repeating in our lonely society of overachievers: relationship with other believers is essential. Community isn't an afterthought for us or a marketing strategy to grow our church. It's who we are. Life was never meant to be lived alone. I need you, and you need me.

Relationship is the core of the gospel itself: God reconciling us to himself through his Son. It's the overarching theme of the Bible. It's the model Jesus gave us for discipleship. It's the pattern the disciples followed in Acts and a central theme repeated throughout the New Testament letters. It's inherent in the images used of the church throughout the Bible: the body of Christ, a family, a household, and the branches of a single vine.

And it will be central in heaven as well. In Revelation, John's vision of heaven involves a feast celebrating the wedding of Jesus and the church, the bride he loved enough to die for. The culmination of redemptive history occurs not in a worship service but at a table.

> Life was never meant to be lived alone. I need you, and you need me.

It is so easy for us to see Christianity in individualistic terms: my relationship with God. But the Bible never does that. When we accept God as our Father, we get adopted into a family. It's not optional. If we want Jesus, we get his family too.

That's messy and complicated and sometimes painful. I don't know about you, but some of the biggest hurts I've experienced have been at the hands of family, either natural or spiritual.

And yet, most of my most precious joys and greatest triumphs have also been in that same context. In times of both joy and sorrow, it is my family I want by my side.

As Christians, we are part of a worldwide family with lives that are intertwined with one another. That is beautiful, precious, and exactly as God intended. We are meant to live in the context of community.

We constantly need to remind ourselves of this. Our culture is fast-paced, goal-focused, and individualistic. If we don't intentionally center our lives around the table of relationship, we will sacrifice the joy and strength of community on the altar of productivity. What a tragedy!

Life at the table means relationship is central to who we are and how we reflect Jesus.

I See You

Life at the table also means that we are committed to being genuine with one another and accepting who the other person really is. It means seeing and being seen.

Truly seeing someone speaks to some of the deepest needs of that person's heart:

> I see you as you are: I value your identity.
> I see you in your pain: I accept you as you are.
> I see you as you will be: I affirm your significance.

There is something in all of us that yearns to be seen. I suspect this is a large part of what drives the popularity of social media, even if the version of ourselves that we post is rarely vulnerable or even real. We yearn to be seen but are afraid that if we show our real selves, we will be rejected, so we create a version of ourselves we think others will admire.

Life at the table means we shed facades and show who we really are. It means we commit to truly seeing and being seen by one another.

We understand the importance of being the real "us" rather than some idealized version designed to impress.

Jesus did this. He was raw and vulnerable with his disciples, willing to be real even if it made them uncomfortable. He shared his discouragement (John 6:67), desperation and grief (Matthew 26:38), frustration (Matthew 17:14-20), and pain (Matthew 27:46). In doing so, he gave them the opportunity to see him and be seen by him. He taught them the real meaning of community.

We are meant to be the same way in our relationships with one another. We are meant to see one another and to be seen.

I'm not talking about using each other as therapists or targets at which to vent our pain. Leveraging a relationship to force someone into bearing our burdens against their will isn't healthy for anyone!

But neither is walling ourselves up so that no one sees the real us, or expecting others to do the same in order to meet our expectations of them. My vision is of a church that reflects the heart of Jesus: unconditional love for one another, a readiness to share in each other's joys and pains, and dedication to mutual growth.

I Love You

Finally, life at the table signifies a commitment to loving one another. That means that we see love not just as an abstract ideal but as a concrete, practical reality that affects how we live our daily lives. I could list dozens, maybe even hundreds, of ways I see love expressed in our community. Every one of them is life-changing for both the giver and the recipient. There are heroes in our church who foster kids and others who support foster parents, volunteers who serve faithfully at Sunday services, people who bring meals to those who are sick, and an entire team that gathers and distributes thousands of presents to needy families every Christmas.

People at all our campuses give selflessly of their time, energy, and resources to bless one another because they love each other. Honestly, there might not be anything besides seeing someone accept Jesus that brings me more joy and gratitude than hearing the stories of people loving people. That is Jesus' heart. That is life at the table.

It's Not Hard

The beautiful thing about life at the table is that it fits naturally into our lives. God isn't asking us to give in to impossible demands on our time or abilities. He's inviting us to simply use what we have to connect with others—to help them, bless them, receive from them, and be strengthened by them.

God doesn't expect you to use skills or gifts you don't possess. You'll probably never see me playing the piano, for example. There is a reason for that! I love you too much to subject you to that kind of torture.

But I do love to cook. So rather than just making a meal for myself or our family, I sometimes invite others over to join us. That takes some planning, energy, and expense. Michal and I have to be intentional about it. But it doesn't feel hard. In fact, we enjoy it deeply.

Life at the table means being intentional about inviting others into your life. It means sharing what you have with them, whatever that is. Often, that is quite literally a table. Inviting others to our homes, accepting an invitation from them, meeting together at a restaurant or café—food is often the catalyst for closer relationships with one another.

But it can be a host of other things as well. Life at the table might mean stopping to chat with your neighbor on your morning walk or when taking out the trash. It might mean mowing their lawn if they need it or offering to feed their pets while they are on vacation. It might mean hosting parties for your kids' friends or opening your home for a church small group. It might mean taking a Saturday to teach a skill you have, such as painting, auto repair, dance, or photography, to someone who wants to learn but has no idea where to start. It might mean inviting someone to church (and picking them up if they need it). It might mean stopping for a couple of minutes to find out how your co-worker is really doing, rather than just tossing a quick "How's it going?" greeting toward them as you rush by to accomplish some task.

Life at the table isn't a program. It's a perspective. It's looking at the world around you—family, friends, neighbors, co-workers, strangers—as people loved by God. It's recognizing that you have something others need and that you have needs they can meet as well. It's shifting deliberately from a self-centered existence to a community-centered one. It's not always simple, and it's countercultural in many Western nations, but it is beautiful. And it is essential if we are really going to disciple others.

One definition we've used in our church that seems to resonate is:

> *Life at the table is the daily, spiritual practice of using our homes, businesses, and everyday lives in a way that seeks to make strangers into friends and friends into the family of God.*

Blessed, Broken, Given

To me, the imagery Jesus used when he sat around a table for the final time with his disciples before his death is more than powerful—it's transformative.

Matthew was one of several disciples who recorded it in his Gospel:

> While they were eating, Jesus took bread, and when he had given thanks, he broke it and gave it to his disciples, saying, "Take and eat; this is my body."
>
> Then he took a cup, and when he had given thanks, he gave it to them, saying, "Drink from it, all of you. This is my blood of the covenant, which is poured out for many for the

> forgiveness of sins. I tell you, I will not drink from this fruit of the vine from now on until that day when I drink it new with you in my Father's kingdom." Matthew (26:27-29)

In his final evening with this small band of disciples whom he'd poured his life into for three years, Jesus didn't just give another sermon. He broke bread with them. He told them that his brokenness would heal their brokenness and his death would bring them life.

That life wasn't meant for them alone, either. His blood was "poured out for many for the forgiveness of sins." John 3:16 says that Jesus' death was for the redemption of the entire world. Anyone who is simply willing to believe can join Jesus at his table. His blood was shed for our healing, and his body was broken to give us life.

Blessed. Broken. Given.

I find that imagery captivating. It speaks first of Jesus' perfect life, his selfless sacrifice on our behalf, and the gift of eternal life to all who believe. But it also echoes in each of our lived experiences. I don't know about you, but I often feel both simultaneously blessed and broken. I'm grateful for all God has done for me but keenly aware of the brokenness that life's trials (and my own choices at times) have caused. It's the painful irony of redeemed life in a sin-shattered world. Blessing and brokenness, healing and heartache, life and loss. I experience them all, often at the same time.

Jesus sees me in this state. He accepts me, loves me, and has a purpose for me in both my blessing and my brokenness. I get to not only receive that love, but to share it with others. I—like Jesus—get to give. That's the essence of the table: sharing in blessing and in brokenness, accepting one another as we are while believing in Jesus' healing power to keep redeeming and restoring each of us, and inviting others to share in the table with us.

I don't think it gets more beautiful than that on this side of heaven.

Questions for Reflection

1. Would you say that the culture you are a part of is individualistic or community-centered? What are some advantages and disadvantages of that?

2. Have you ever felt truly "seen" by someone else? What did they do or say that communicated this? Do you have relationships in your life now where you can see and be seen?

3. After reading this chapter, what about "life at the table" is most meaningful to you? Has God given you any ideas about how you could share your life with others? What would the first step of obedience toward that look like?

Chapter 8

LITTLE MOMENTS MEAN THE MOST

Time off from the routine of work, school, and life's daily responsibilities has always been a priority for my wife and me. Even when we were younger and our finances were at times precarious, I would work side gigs to pay for trips to the coast or central Oregon and occasionally for longer trips to different states and countries.

Sometime after our second child was born, I surprised my wife with a trip to Hawaii. It would be our first time there, and I just knew she'd be as excited as I was.

When I announced the good news, however, her response was considerably less enthusiastic than I had imagined it would be. At first, I assumed she just thought it was too good to believe. I'd spent a month's wages on this trip, and I was expecting her to be thrilled. But later that night, when I asked her how she felt about the upcoming trip, her response stunned me. She said, "I just don't think it's that big of a deal. I'd rather just stay home with our kids for a week and have some friends over for dinner and games."

We talked for a while, and I came to see the trip from her perspective. The idea of leaving behind our two small kids, traveling across the ocean, learning to navigate a new city and state, and spending so much money did not excite her. To her, it just sounded like more stress. That had never been my intention at all, of course, but it was her reality.

After considering all the options, we forged ahead. We enjoyed our time and were glad we went. But upon returning home, one of the first things we did, besides collecting our kids from grandma and grandpa's house, was invite a group of friends over. We made chili dogs with Nathan's hot dogs and, yes, chili from a can. While our kids played (and created a mess beyond explanation) in the background, we ate simple food and played Yahtzee together. That night proved much richer, more fulfilling, and more valuable than the entire eight-day trip across the ocean.

I learned a valuable lesson through that: bigger isn't always better, and costly isn't always valuable. The simple act of spending time with friends turned out to be more meaningful than my elaborate and expensive plans.

The Little Moments

If you made a list of the most meaningful moments of your life—the moments that changed your view of yourself or the course of your life forever—what would they be? Chances are, most of them were unplanned, inexpensive, and maybe not even all that meaningful to others who were involved. But for you, they were life-changing. An encouraging word, a suggestion of a job you could look into, a gentle (or maybe not-so-gentle) rebuke when you were headed toward a metaphorical cliff at high speed, a thoughtful gift, wise counsel when you didn't know what to do...the list could go on and on.

In the last chapter, I highlighted how central the idea of "life at the table" is in Christian experience and community. One of the primary reasons that this kind of living is so powerful is that it provides the context for these little moments that mean the most to occur. Such moments are rarely planned, prepared, or part of an intentional strategy. They are simply spontaneous words or actions shared between people who care for one another that are used by God in ways we could never have anticipated.

Parenting experts used to discuss the value of "quality" time parents should have with kids versus "quantity" time. The idea was that a few key interactions could be more powerful than many hours of unplanned time.

It's a great theory—until you have kids. Then you realize that children are rarely (in my experience, it's more like never) open to a deep, meaningful conversation when you've scheduled time for it. They want to talk at totally random times, often ones that aren't particularly convenient.

I'm not an expert at parenting. I've had enough experience to know how much I don't know! Like most parents, I'm a lot less dogmatic now about parenting techniques than I was before I had kids. But one thing I am convinced of: you don't get quality time without quantity time. Those random, priceless interactions occur when we prioritize time together consistently, generously, and authentically.

That concept holds true across the spectrum of relationships. The more time you spend with your kids, your spouse, your family, your friends, and your community, the more opportunities you'll have for those unplanned, priceless little moments where God uses a word or action to forever change someone's life.

I've seen this countless times in my life. I've been both the giver and the receiver of words or actions that were divinely orchestrated. Sometimes I had a plan in those moments. But more often, I didn't have a plan (or I *did* have a plan, but God blew that one up and then revealed his own, infinitely better, one instead).

Seeing God's Hand in It All

If we have eyes to see, we will recognize God's handiwork everywhere. Every moment we live is a gift from God that he uses for good.

We aren't passive recipients in this process, however. God wants to bless us, but he also wants to bless the world through us. He uses our words and actions to show his love to others.

That means that everything we do ought to be viewed as sacred. God can and does use the most insignificant, ridiculous, and even embarrassing things we do to bless both us and the people around us. We don't know what word or action might prove to be a life-changing moment for someone we are interacting with. God uses it all for his glory and our good.

Life at the table, then, isn't just about enjoying life together. It's about recognizing that the eternal purposes of God can be fulfilled in and through every action we take. Whether we are at home, at work, with friends, or at church, everything we do matters to God because he uses it all for good.

> Most of what God does happens outside the walls of the church rather than inside, simply because that's where we spend most of our lives.

Looking at life this way infuses it with beauty and purpose. A friend of mine likes to say, "Everyone is an artist in some way." We tend to think of art as a painting, a photograph, or some other creation made purely for the sake of its beauty or originality. Artists, photographers, videographers, and similar types of people get the label "creative." But there is an artistry—a creativity, a beauty, and an elegance—to so many other kinds of work that fall outside the category of traditional art. Spend time with someone who writes code for apps or software, and you'll see it. Look at the work of a skilled electrician, contractor, or barista, and it's evident. Even a well-designed spreadsheet reflects it! Artistry is built into who we are and how we express ourselves because God is creative and the creator of beauty itself.

In the same way that my friend sees beauty and artistry in what others call ordinary, we need to be able to see God's beautiful purposes in even the mundane moments that might seem insignificant to others. God's purposes aren't just fulfilled through the preacher or worship team on a Sunday morning. In fact, most of what God does happens outside the walls of the church rather than inside, simply because that's where we spend most of our lives. And God has chosen to use us to accomplish his purposes in this world.

He's picked you and I, along with every other unqualified but willing person in his messy family, to be his ambassadors to this world. We're his messengers every day, everywhere we go. We represent him, and that means everything we do has the potential to reflect and reveal who he is.

This is inspiring and freeing. It removes the mundane from everyday life and replaces it with sacredness and potential. It infuses our work, our errands, and every other aspect of our existence with the beauty of purpose.

But it can also feel a bit overwhelming. If God reveals himself to the world—or at least wants to—through us all the time, then what are we supposed to do about that? Do we write up a doctoral thesis on how we are going to maximize our personal potential, stressing out about our responsibility to show God's love to the world? Or do we go to the opposite extreme and slide into passiveness, expecting God to do his thing without us playing any intentional part?

Fortunately, there's a middle path between those two, a path that may feel surprisingly natural and stress-free. Yes, it requires intentionality on your part—you do have to move toward others. But it doesn't require you to be someone you aren't or act in ways that feel forced. It's called B.L.E.S.S.

B.L.E.S.S.

One of the most helpful models I've found for how to live my life intentionally while avoiding overthinking everything is an approach developed by Pastor Dave Ferguson called B.L.E.S.S. It's a simple acronym that stands for the following progression:

B – Begin with Prayer
L – Listen
E – Eat
S – Serve
S – Story

This way of approaching interactions with others can transform the way you think about your time, your place in your community, and how God might be able to use you to help others in ways you could never have expected.

B - Begin with prayer

Jesus came to find people who are lost and to help those who are hurting. As we seek to join him in his mission, we begin with prayer, recognizing we can only do this through God's power.

Ask God where he wants you to join him in the work he is doing in your family, friends, and others in your community. Make it more than a perfunctory prayer that you don't expect an answer to. Ask him to speak to you!

If you're not sure where to start, here are some questions to ask. You might be surprised how faithful God is to drop thoughts or insights into your mind when you ask specific questions and genuinely want to do his will.

- "Father, what gifts or abilities have you given me? Can I use any of those to bless someone today?
- "Is there anyone in my circle who is hurting? Could you guide me in how to bring your comfort to them?"
- "Are there distractions in my life that are keeping me focused on myself rather than on others? How do you want me to handle those distractions today?"
- "Is there anyone I could invite over for a meal or show hospitality to in some way this week?"
- "Is something making my life feel so full that I have no time to think about or care for others? What should I do about it?"
- "Are there people you want me to pray for regularly? Who?"

I'd suggest keeping a journal or notes app handy so that for each of these questions (plus any others you might ask), you can write down what you feel God is saying to you. This can help you clarify what you are feeling and hearing. It is also a way to remember God's assignment for you this week, and in the future, it will be a testimony of how God used you to help those around you.

L - Listen

This second step is one that is surprisingly difficult for many of us to do, even though it sounds simple. As a society, we are not particularly good at listening. We might like to be the center of attention, or we could feel awkward at a momentary silence in the room, or we may subconsciously become so eager to fix others' problems that we forget how essential it is to truly hear them.

David Augsberger said, "Being heard is so close to being loved that for the average person, they are almost indistinguishable."[10] When we listen to people, we communicate something of far greater value than any sage advice we could give them: we tell them, in a way that our words couldn't, that they matter. That they are valuable. That their story is worth telling. That what they have to say is more important than our agenda.

That doesn't mean our words have no value. In fact, God can and will give you words of wisdom, insight, and even prophetic understanding to help you speak life into people. But rarely will that happen up front. Any wisdom you have to share will be immeasurably helped (and more likely to be accepted) if you start by listening.

Jesus often engaged people by asking them questions and loving them through conversation. When people are heard and understood, they feel safe and valued. So get curious and ask good questions. Listen deeply to people's dreams and pain. What's more, listen for evidence of God's work in their lives so you can participate in the work God is already doing. Listen well so you can learn how to bless others!

Here are some questions you can ask yourself to help you start engaging the people around you in conversation. Just remember: the primary goal is to listen so that you can really get to know them, so avoid dominating the conversation. Learn the art of listening, and you will change lives.

Questions for where you live:
- Do you know the names of your neighbors? How can you introduce yourself?
- Who is elderly or disabled? What might they need help with?
- Who could you invite over to your home for a meal?
- Who has moved in recently? How could you help welcome them to the neighborhood?

Questions for where you work:
- Is there someone at your workplace or school who doesn't fit in, is different, or gets bullied? How can you help them feel loved and valued?
- Do you know of any birthdays, anniversaries, or other special events that are happening? How could you help someone celebrate?
- Do any of your coworkers hang out together after work? How can you join in or initiate a gathering?
- Is there a coworker who always goes out of their way to help or serve you? How could you acknowledge their kindness or express your thanks?

Questions for where you play:
- Where do you go frequently, such as the gym, library, sporting events, restaurants, bars, or shops? How can you get to know the people you see frequently at this place?
- Can you take opportunities to make a casual encounter something more? It may be a barista, bartender, someone checking you in at the gym, or the person running beside you on the treadmill.

- How can you listen and express care for the people with whom you regularly interact?
- How can you make this place a better and more positive one?

E - Eat with others

Some things are just better together, like peanut butter and jelly. It is also true of the two practices of listening and eating. Why do these make such a powerful combo? First, because neighbors seldom share meals together. In our individualistic society, hospitality is an extravagant gesture of goodwill. Second, when the meal is centered on good conversation to get to know your neighbor, it comes across as a tremendously generous act. Much of Jesus' ministry involved conversations around a table. Active listening coupled with a good meal can catapult a casual acquaintance into a growing friendship.

The meal doesn't have to be a feast. The house doesn't have to be spotless. Your kids don't have to pretend they don't have a sin nature. You're not inviting people over to observe your performance or admire your production—you're inviting them over to share life with them.

Hospitality can be (and usually is) very simple. The people I know who love hospitality don't feel obligated to impress people. They just want to serve them.

If you can't cook, invite someone over for coffee or dessert. Or pick a meal you'd like to know how to cook, then ask if they want to come over and make it together. Get creative and don't be afraid to fail. Some of my favorite memories involve events that didn't go as planned. They tend to make the most vivid memories (and the best stories), in part because the spontaneity that results from unexpected difficulties can be incredibly bonding.

Chances are, as you've been reading this, a name or two has come to mind—someone you could invite over for a meal or dessert. Maybe the thought has been inspiring and you're excited to try it.

Great! Maybe it sounds overwhelming. That's alright too. But don't let nervousness stop you from leaning into what God wants to do through you. Give it a try! See what God might do.

S - Serve

This part of the model focuses on how we can serve those around us in practical ways. Service will look very different in different contexts, which is why it comes after "Eat" in this model. This doesn't mean we can't serve someone until we've shared a meal. It just reflects the fact that we usually get a better idea of how to serve others the more we get to know them. We may find out during that meal how we can be a help or encouragement to our neighbors in ways that are natural, unforced, and greatly appreciated. But the same thing can also happen through a thoughtful conversation (remember, this should involve a lot of listening!) while you're doing yard work or if you stop to chat while on a walk.

Often we are so focused on our own lives that we don't think about others that much. It's not that we're intentionally selfish; it's more that we haven't learned to get in the habit of thinking *out* rather than just *in*.

Here are a few questions to help you get started. As you read these, ask yourself if you know the answers to any of them about your neighbors, co-workers, or others in your community. If so, look for relevant ways to serve them. If not, use this list of questions to help you be more intentional in your next conversation. These are just to get you thinking—don't use this as a checklist or the conversation will sound like an interrogation. The goal isn't to stalk someone or be intrusive; it's to get to know the other person and show that you genuinely care and want to help. So use your God-given wisdom and depend on the Holy Spirit to help you ask the right questions at the right time. Remember that he loves them more than you do and knows them better than you ever will. You can trust him to help you.

How is my neighbor doing relationally?
- How is their home life?
- How is their marriage, dating, or family life going?
- Do they have close friends?
- How are their relationships at work?

How is my neighbor doing physically?
- How is their overall health?
- Are they getting regular exercise?
- Are their eating habits healthy?
- Do they mention not being able to sleep?

How is my neighbor doing mentally and emotionally?
- Are there any signs of anxiety?
- Is there any indication of depression?
- Have I noticed any mood swings?
- Are there any unhealthy thought patterns showing up?

How is my neighbor doing spiritually?
- Do they sense something is missing in their life?
- Are they willing to have me pray for them?
- Do they display a spiritual curiosity?
- Do they initiate spiritual conversation?

S - Story

The final part of the B.L.E.S.S. model is *story*. This refers to your life, your experiences, and your encounter with God. It's incredibly powerful because a story has a way of getting past people's analytical, defensive barriers and right into their hearts. Jesus used stories constantly when he was teaching. His parables captured people's imaginations and illustrated truth in ways that a sermon never could. Modern-day marketing gurus recognize the power of stories, which is why products being sold so often include testimonials or user reviews.

And they're right. When I'm researching a product on Amazon, I peruse the reviews to see what actual customers have to say about the product, and you probably do as well.

Your story carries weight with others. Your lived experience proves that the Bible's message is relevant and true today. This is especially true if you *aren't* a pastor! People assume that pastors will say that the Bible is true, God is good, and everyone should go to church. (The cynical ones even assume we're selling that message as a means to get more people into our church who will give money.) But when you—their neighbor, co-worker, or friend with no supposed ulterior motive—testify about the power and love of God in your own life, people listen without defensiveness or suspicion.

You don't have to have a dramatic testimony, by the way. Growing up, I heard lots of powerful stories from people whose lives had been crime-ridden, violent, abusive, and disastrous before God rescued them. The stories were exciting, but to be honest they left me feeling a little disappointed in my own! God's power in my life had mostly been demonstrated in protection from harm, not rescue from it. But I've come to realize that doesn't mean my story is boring to others. Every day I face the same issues others do: uncertainties, setbacks, opportunities, decisions, relational challenges, etc. And every day I see God's hand help and comfort me as I navigate those. In reality, dramatic stories of a crime-filled past wouldn't be as relevant to most of my neighbors as the daily faithfulness of God helping me be the kind of husband, father, and neighbor that I want to be.

> Your story can change lives in ways you could never imagine.

"Story" comes last in this model for two reasons. First, we tend to talk too much about ourselves, and this is a healthy reminder that we need to do more listening and serving than talking! Second, our story will carry much more weight when it's told in the context of a relationship. My friends care more about my experiences and my perspectives than random strangers do. That's just how it works.

Chances are, you won't have to wonder when it's time to tell your story. As you get to know someone, they will ask. They'll want to know your experience as well as your wisdom, because they will have come to know you and even trust you. It will feel natural, unforced, and relational. But it will be more than that. It will be infused with God's purposes and empowered by his Spirit. Your story can change lives in ways you could never imagine.

Your story is powerful. One simple way to see this more clearly and to be prepared if the chance comes to share your story with others is to think through how Jesus has made a difference in your life. Having an answer to this will help you "always be prepared to give an answer to everyone who asks you to give the reason for the hope that you have" (1 Peter 3:15). To do that, take a minute (right now, if you can), and think through these questions:

1. **My life before Jesus.** What was your life like before you met Jesus? Or, if you grew up in church, what was it like before you developed a close relationship with him and became serious about following him? What emotions dominated your life? How did you seek purpose, happiness, or peace? How did you handle problems or crises?

2. **How I met Jesus.** How did you become a Christ-follower? Was there a friend or family member who was influential? Was there a particular experience or series of experiences that inspired you to get closer to God?

3. **My life since I met Jesus**. What difference has following Jesus made in your life? How has knowing him impacted how you walk through both the exciting times and the hard times in life? Shar e the good and the bad when telling your story. People will be more impacted when you're honest about the challenges you continue to face even since choosing to follow Jesus. And don't

give the easy Sunday School answer. Talk about how your life is different and how God is helping you grow in various areas, but make sure you're sincere about how it's still a process. Be as real with others as you would like them to be with you.

Let the answers to those questions be the starting point for you on a journey of self-reflection. God has done more miracles for you than you probably realize. Time spent on this exercise will likely be a real encouragement to you as well as being beneficial to others in your life. Who knows how many people might someday think of you as that friend or family member who helped point them to Jesus?

Questions for Reflection

1. What are a couple of the most meaningful moments you can remember in your own life? How did they affect you?

2. The B.L.E.S.S. model (Begin with Prayer, Listen, Eat, Serve, Story) provides a framework for being intentional about your interactions with others. Which part feels like it would be the easiest for you? Which feels like it would be the most challenging? Why?

3. We all have a story about how Jesus has transformed our lives. What is yours? How might it help other people?

THE FUNDAMENTALS OF MOVEMENT

God's purpose in all this was to use the church to display his wisdom in its rich variety to all the unseen rulers and authorities in the heavenly places. This was his eternal plan, which he carried out through Christ Jesus our Lord. Because of Christ and our faith in him, we can now come boldly and confidently into God's presence. So please don't lose heart because of my trials here. I am suffering for you, so you should feel honored.
Ephesians 3:10–13 NLT

First rule of change is controversy. You can't get away from it for the simple reason that all issues are controversial. Change means movement, and movement means friction, and friction means heat, and heat means controversy.
—Saul Alinsky

Chapter 9

THE CALL

M y family always had a large garden when I was young. My
parents grew a lot of different varieties of vegetables, but
one of my favorites was the green beans. Although we
lived in the Pacific Northwest, both my parents were originally from
the mountains of North Carolina. There was something about North
Carolina beans that just tasted better than anything we could get in the
PNW, so my parents faithfully ordered seeds out of a mail-order cat-
alog (I just dated myself for sure) and had them sent to us every year.

One year when I was ten years old, I decided I wanted my own
bean patch. My dad rototilled a plot of ground for me, and I got to
work. I remember being so proud and excited as I laid out the rows,
drove cedar stakes in the ground to mark the ends of the rows, and
then planted the bean seeds in the soil.

I went to bed sure that night sure that the next morning I'd see
bean plants sprouting. Early the next morning, I ran out to see them.
NOTHING. The second and third days yielded the same disappointing
results. I was too young to understand how much time was needed for
seeds to germinate, but I was old enough to know that water would
help. So, I headed to the shed, grabbed a can, and filled it with water.

For several days I faithfully watered that patch, but nothing happened. Eventually, even my dad grew puzzled at the lack of growth. I
explained that I'd watered them and everything, but with no results.
My dad looked at me strangely, then asked me what I'd used to pour
water on the garden. And that's the day I learned a valuable gardening
tip: you can't use a gas can to water beans. I hadn't been watering the
soil; I'd been poisoning it!

Needless to say, I didn't get a crop that year. But I did get a lesson. Sincerity and even hard work aren't enough to bring a vision to reality. You can have a great idea and lots of faith, but it's what you do next that matters. *How* we move in response to God's voice is vital.

In the first section of this book, we explored the truth that *we are created to move*: designed by God to respond to his calling on our lives with intentionality and faith. That's why movement comes so naturally to us and why responding to God is vital.

In the second section, we looked at our model for movement: *life at the table*. Movement isn't meant to be robotic or artificial but natural and relational. The way we respond to God and partner with him is by letting him infuse our daily lives with purpose.

In this third section, I want to look at the *mechanics of movement*. We know God wants to work in and through us. We understand that we are created to move, and we are eager to do just that. But we don't want to pour gasoline on our bean patch! So what does it mean to respond, and how does that work out practically in our lives?

To better understand the mechanics of movement, I want to return to Abraham's life. The ways that God interacted with him reveal patterns and principles that are still relevant today.

When God Calls

The first element in this process is one that we see repeated over and over throughout Scripture and history, because it is what prompts movement in the first place: the divine call of God.

Remember, Abraham was living comfortably in the town of Terah with his family when God upended his life, giving him a mandate to leave home and head out into the unknown. There weren't a lot of details given in that initial command, just a challenge and a promise. The challenge was to move; the promise was that through Abraham, God would bless not just him and his family but every nation of the world.

We don't know how God communicated to Abraham. If it was something dramatic, such as a visit from an angel, the Bible doesn't say that. It's interesting that later on in his story, when angels do show up, the Bible describes that in detail. So my guess is that in this situation, Abraham heard God the same way you and I sometimes do: an inner prompting, a quiet voice in our spirit, a "knowing" in our mind that the thought we just had was not our own.

> Movement always begins with a thought. God's voice causes us to think, to wonder, to imagine what the future could become.

Movement always begins with a thought. God's voice causes us to think, to wonder, to imagine what the future could become. I'm sure Abraham had plenty of thoughts when he first felt God's Spirit challenging him to leave home. And when he brought the idea up to his wife Sarah, she probably had a few thoughts of her own. Leaving the city they knew, where God had blessed them, must have seemed a little crazy.

But Abraham knew God had spoken. It had been clear enough that he could recite the very words of the command. And he made the decision to obey.

There have been times in my life when I've known I was hearing the call of God and that I needed to respond. I've sat with the knowledge that God was calling me to leave my place of comfort and blessing and follow him into the unknown. I've contemplated the risks, the challenges, the ways it could go wrong, and the rewards. I've wondered if I was hearing correctly or not. I've talked it over with my wife and others I love, listening to their concerns and hearing in their doubts an echo of my own fear. But like Abraham and Sarah, Michal and I have chosen to take those steps into the unknown time and time again in response to God's call.

Has there been a time in your life when you knew God was directing you? Do you remember the fear, the doubt, the excitement? How did you respond? How will you respond when he calls you the next time? These are questions worth asking yourself. If you have ever moved in obedience to God, you probably have stories of your own that testify to God's power and wisdom. Those stories are part of your past but also part of your future because they will help strengthen your faith the next time God speaks. They will be part of the story of your life that you share to encourage others.

If you know God called you to do something at some point in the past, but you didn't move in response for one reason or another, don't let shame or doubt creep in and rob you of the peace God wants to give you. Your story isn't over yet. God is faithful, patient, and merciful. He knows we don't get it right every time, and he still loves us.

In fact, if there's one thing we learn from the stories of Israel in the Old Testament, it's that God is patient with our faults. The Israelites saw God's power and mercy firsthand as he brought them out of Egypt, but they doubted him over and over. They questioned his words, his goodness, and his plan. They complained and whined and bickered. And yet, God kept leading them. He was faithful even when they were faithless. Despite all they did to go off track, God kept bringing them back and continued leading them to the land he'd promised them. In fact, the only reason they didn't inherit that land in the end was that when they arrived, they flat-out refused to enter. God didn't disqualify them; they disqualified themselves. Even then, God didn't give up on them. He simply transferred the promises to the next generation of Israelites, a generation who would believe him and move in response to his call. So take heart. God is ready and willing to give you another opportunity, regardless of your past.

When God Whispers

Sometimes, the call of God is clear and undeniable. We "know that we know" he is speaking to us. Our dilemma isn't whether we're hearing him correctly but whether we have the faith to respond.

But in my experience, that kind of call is relatively rare. As far as we know, God only spoke in a clear, dramatic fashion to Abraham a few times in his whole life. And yet, God was leading him constantly. I can think of a handful of times in my life when God's calling was crystal clear in the moment. But I can think of hundreds of times when I made a decision or a move that only in hindsight proved to be divinely ordained.

The vast majority of the time, God leads us in far more subtle ways than a booming voice from heaven, a dramatic sign, or a prophetic word. Mostly, God whispers. We wake up one morning with an idea. We get a thought we can't shake. We hear a sermon or a song whose words resonate with an unspoken yearning in our hearts. We feel an urge we can't explain to do something.

Not all of these thoughts, ideas, and desires come from God, of course. The Bible is clear that we need to use wisdom and discernment. Saying "God told me" to justify every idea we have is not going to glorify God or work out well for us.

But I believe that more of those dreams and ideas are God-breathed than we often realize. I think we need to start seeing more of our thoughts as being divinely inspired. Rather than dismissing every out-of-the-box idea as too crazy, too risky, or too bold, we need to take them seriously.

Our God is creative, wise, original, loving, and purposeful, and I am absolutely convinced that he wants to put ideas into our minds that reflect those characteristics. Our churches ought to be full of entrepreneurs, creatives, artists, groundbreakers and trailblazers, people who bring a prophetic edge to everything they do.

I've talked to countless businesspeople who share my passion for the world to know Jesus but who know their grace gift is for marketplace leadership rather than traditional "full-time ministry." As a pastor, that thrills me. I have friends whose business acumen has opened doors for them to work with CEOs, celebrities, and people whose net worth is more than my entire neighborhood. And because they love Jesus and are committed to his mission, they are able to share his love with people who would otherwise never listen. The same could be said for doctors, construction workers, teachers, administrators, retail support workers, and more.

When I listen to friends talk about the doors God has opened for them and the risks they took to go through those doors, it is abundantly clear that God called them, they responded to the challenge, and he blessed them as a result.

Learning to Hear

God speaks to us in many different ways. Whether we are listening or not is the real question! As the book of Job puts it, "For God does speak—now one way, now another—though no one perceives it" (33:14).

Here are just a few ways he communicated to people in the Bible. These are ways he continues to use today if we are open to hearing him.

> Scripture (2 Timothy 3:16-17)
> Inner witness (Romans 8:16)
> Jesus' life and words (Hebrews 1:1-2)
> Prophecy (1 Corinthians 14:1-25)
> The quiet voice of the Holy Spirit (John 14:26)
> Dreams and visions (Acts 16:9)
> The words of other people (1 Thessalonians 2:13; 1 Samuel 3:9)
> Songs and poetry (Colossians 3:16)
> Angels (Acts 8:26)
> Nature (Psalm 19:1-2; Romans 1:20)
> History (Acts 17:26-28)

I suspect God is talking to us far more than we realize. We're too busy, too distracted, or just too oblivious to the idea that he'd even want to speak to us for us to listen. But what would happen if we slowed down and really made hearing from God our priority? I can tell you. We'd begin to hear his call. We'd begin to be aware more than ever before of his purpose and our part in it.

A common question people have at this point is, "How do I know if I'm really hearing God?" Maybe an idea or a thought has come to you, but you aren't sure if it's a God-inspired plan or a disaster waiting to happen. After all, unless the message was literally delivered by an angel, you may well wonder if what you're sensing is really God's voice.

If that's you, know that the doubt you're feeling is actually a good thing! It means you want to get it right. It means you aren't trying to use God's calling as a way to justify your own ambition. You want to hear him accurately because your goal is obedience. That's a wonderful place to start.

But while initial uncertainty can be helpful in reminding us to stay humble, I believe we can grow to discern God's leading more and more clearly. We can become confident that we are hearing him, and we can step out and make bold moves because we know God has spoken to us. There is no magic formula for it, but here are some things I've learned in my own journey.

Let me unpack these briefly because this is important. Your ability to discern God's voice can save you from heartache, moral failures, and financial ruin. It can help you live the life of peace and blessing that you yearn to experience.

1. **You'll get it wrong sometimes.** As much as I wish there was a fool-proof way to know we're hearing God's voice correctly, there isn't one. We're finite humans with a penchant for stubbornness and self-deceit. We're going to mess up sometimes. I don't say this to discourage you. In fact, I hope it does the opposite. If you get it wrong once in a while (or more than that), you're in good company! All of us are feeling our way through life. It's okay not to know everything. It keeps us humble (we'll

talk about that in a minute) and dependent on God's daily leading. Sometimes you'll hear God correctly. Other times you won't. Thankfully...

2. **God is sovereign anyway.** One of the clearest teachings in the Bible is the sovereignty of God. God directs our steps (Proverbs 16:9), influences political leaders (Proverbs 21:1), sets the course of nations (Acts 17:26-28), controls nature (Psalm 135:6-7), and gives us the desire to do what is right (Philippians 2:13). He not only sees our mistakes, but he also anticipates them and turns them into good. One of the most well-known verses in the Bible is "And we know that God causes everything to work together for the good of those who love God and are called according to his purpose for them" (Romans 8:28, NLT). It's famous because it's so encouraging. God's will won't be derailed by my stupidity, weakness, or failure. He will pick me up, set me back on track, then use even my mistakes to accomplish his purposes.

3. **Keep your heart humble and committed to God.** Humility, teachability, and the earnest desire to obey God are foundational to hearing his voice. King David said, "[The LORD] guides the humble in what is right and teaches them his way... Who then, are those who fear the LORD? he will instruct them in the ways they should choose" (Psalm 25:9,12). There is no better safeguard than humility and no greater danger than pride.

4. **God's Word is the standard by which all other words must be judged.** The Bible is our authority. If what you are sensing is in line with Scripture, it may be from God. If it contradicts Scripture, it isn't. I heard a story once of a man who was contemplating leaving his wife. So he prayed that if it was God's will, God would turn all the traffic lights green on his way to work that day. The lights were all green, so the man divorced his wife. I

don't care if the traffic lights turn purple. You don't get to put your own desires above the Word of God! Every time you feel you might be hearing from God, it should drive you back to the Bible for confirmation or correction.

5. **Get confirmation before you do anything dramatic.** Paul told the Corinthian church that whenever anyone prophesies, the others should "weigh carefully what is said" (1 Corinthians 14:29). Proverbs gives similar advice in the area of decision-making in general: "The way of fools seems right to them, but the wise listen to advice" (12:15). If you're married, listen to your spouse! This doesn't mean to ignore your own thoughts and turn over all decision-making to them, but it does mean to take very seriously the concerns they may have. After all, God is probably speaking to them too, and almost always, the wisest path will be the one you choose together. Others who are likely to give good counsel are parents, mentors, and spiritual leaders. Friends can be invaluable as well, but they can also tend to rubber-stamp your ideas out of bias or fear of offending you. When getting counsel, look for people who love you more than they love your approval.

6. **Be willing to adapt as you go.** God rarely, if ever, gives us a complete map of the future. Usually it's an idea of the goal and a peace about the next step. The rest is often vague. None of us likes uncertainty, so we tend to fill in that uncertain future with our own ideas. Some of those may be right, but often they aren't. So, be willing to adapt as you go. Uncertainty is disorientating and stressful. But it is a great way to stay humble and dependent on God!

7. **Learn from your mistakes.** The journey of learning to hear and respond to God's voice will not be perfect. You will occasionally mishear, misunderstand, or fail to respond correctly. That's not the end of the journey. Someone once said, "The only way

the devil wins is if we quit." So don't quit. If you make a fool of yourself, at least you did it for Jesus' sake! Apologize if you need to, learn from your mistake, and carry on. But don't judge your thought to be a failure too quickly, either. Some seeds take longer than others to grow, and what you call failure might just be a seed that needs some more time to bear fruit. Either way, don't be discouraged. Proverbs says, "For though the righteous fall seven times, they rise again" (24:16). Failure isn't fatal (unless you're skydiving, I suppose), so ask God to help you figure out why you misheard him and how to improve.

God is calling you to join his movement, to have a purpose beyond yourself, and to hear and respond to his calling on your life. If you are willing to do that, the journey begins. Like Abraham, you are destined to step outside of what is comfortable and safe in order to walk a journey that will bring blessing to the world around you.

Questions for Reflection _____

1. Have you ever had a good idea or goal, but the way you went about it kept you from getting the results you expected? What did you learn from that experience?

2. In what ways does God usually speak to you? When is it easiest to hear his voice? When is it hardest?

3. If you think you might be hearing from God, how do you seek confirmation? What mentors or friends do you trust to speak truth and wisdom when you need to hear it?

Chapter 10

THE STAGES

have a friend who recently started climbing mountains. He calls it "fun." The Pacific Northwest is a breathtakingly beautiful region with numerous snow-capped peaks surrounding Portland, and my friend has summited several of them in the past year or so. When I see his photos on social media, I think two things: "What an amazing view," and "I'm so glad he's doing that and not me." My own hobbies involve a significantly lower chance of getting hypothermia or falling off a mountain, and I'm okay with that.

Shortly after my friend started climbing things, he set his sights on Mt. Hood, the tallest mountain in Oregon and one that requires stamina and some technical climbing equipment and skills. The first thing he did was get a large photo of Mt. Hood and an actual ice ax. He hung both on the wall of his office, where he'd see them every day, in order to keep the vision fresh and motivate himself to train.

Then, he started preparing. Over the course of the next year, he did numerous smaller climbs to build his physical fitness, spent time learning mountaineering skills from more experienced climbers, and, piece by piece, accumulated the gear he needed to make the climb. A few months ago, he successfully summited Mt. Hood. Now he's going through a similar process to train for Mt. Rainier.

If you've ever set your sights on a goal that was bigger than what you could accomplish immediately, you may have done something like that. You figured out the steps you'd need to take and began tackling them one at a time. Then, you kept the vision in front of you as you moved from stage to stage in the fulfillment of it.

God works in a very similar way in our lives. He knows what he intends to accomplish in and through us. He has a vision for our lives, one that is bigger and more beautiful than anything we could conjure up on our own. And he leads us, step by step, toward the fulfillment of that vision.

We get a view of that vision, or a part of it at least, when he calls us to step out of our comfort zone and move toward something he's revealed to us. And more often than not, this movement takes place in distinct stages. (We sometimes speak of seasons, but the concept is the same.) God's character never changes, regardless of the stage. However, the way he chooses to work in us and what he focuses on while he does his work may change. God is always moving, which means we are too.

Understanding the idea of stages can be tremendously encouraging as we move in response to God's call. It provides perspective, develops perseverance, and helps us see our progress en route to the promise of God we are pursuing. It also helps us partner with God as we discern what he's focusing on in and through our lives in the different seasons.

First Steps Stage

Abraham's life after he responded to God's call reflects this concept of stages. Genesis 12:9 says, "Then Abraham continued traveling south by stages toward the Negev" (NLT). While we probably won't literally replicate his journey through a desert to obey God's call, we can learn a lot from how God directed Abraham during each stage.

The first stage began when Abraham heard God's call and responded to it by gathering his family, packing up his possessions, and saying goodbye to his father and community.

When Abraham took his first step into the sandy desert, with nothing in front of him but unending vistas of more sand, he must have felt a bit overwhelmed. The moment was certainly pivotal to his destiny, and he knew it. A step is one of the most powerful moments in a person's life, after all. It is a victory over the force of inertia exerted by the past and the present. It is a conscious decision to embrace the risk of the unknown because we know the character and power of the One who has called us to take that step. It's a commitment, and our lives will never be the same.

> A step is one of the most powerful moments in a person's life.

This stage is one of excitement, imagination, vision, fear, and adrenaline. If you've ever launched a business, decided to marry the person you loved, moved across the country or overseas, bought a home, started a new job, or committed yourself in some other way to a new path in life, you know exactly what this feels like. It's exciting and terrifying at the same time. There's a sense of partnership with God and dependence on him that is indescribably comforting.

In this stage, lean into that dependence on God! Listen for his voice. Write down what you hear because his words to you in this moment will sustain you in the difficult stages to come. The call will be tested, not once but many times, and you will need to cling tightly to the words you heard God say before you took your first step.

As well as depending on God, seek confirmation from others you trust so you are confident you are hearing God correctly. Sometimes we get the call right but the timing is wrong. Other times our own fears, biases, or ambition cause us to misinterpret some aspect of God's call. He will often use the wisdom of others to help guide us.

During this stage, the excitement of promised adventure is often punctuated by times of fear (at least if you're honest enough to stop and think about how you really feel). That's normal. Life has real risks and real consequences for mistakes, so wisdom and caution go hand in hand. When you are in this first stage of moving in response to God's call, don't deny the fear that may be present. But don't let it rule, either. Fear is a God-given gift if kept in its place. It alerts us to potential danger and motivates us to be alert and take care how we act. That's a good thing!

The Bible often tells us to fear the Lord, for example. In fact, Proverbs says that is the beginning of wisdom (Proverbs 1:7). This doesn't mean we have an unreasonable terror of God—he's a good Father whose character and love we can trust completely. It means we are to have a healthy fear of the consequences of disobeying him. Healthy fear recognizes the potential negative consequences of foolish actions and helps us choose wisdom instead. But fear should never derail our trust in God

A good rule of thumb when you're trying to discern your own heart attitude is this: fear that encourages you to stick close to God is healthy; fear that tempts you to abandon God's call is not.

Advancement Stages

Abraham's journey of faith went well at first. Genesis 12:4-6 lists the towns and campsites he visited. God himself appeared to Abraham at one point and promised that the land where Abraham was would one day belong to his descendants. Two different times, Abraham stopped to build an altar and worship. While God had not yet given Abraham possession of the land, he was clearly blessing Abraham's journey and giving him success.

When we respond to God and take those first steps, we will usually see stages of advancement. Sometimes, one happens right away, which is always encouraging. Other times, a stage of testing comes first (we'll get to that one shortly), before advancement. Most of the time, the two stages alternate—for a while, we feel like we are making great progress, then suddenly we hit a roadblock, then God opens a door and we make some more progress, then another trial comes out of nowhere, etc.

Whatever order the stages show up, the advancement stage will come, and it's fun! It is indescribably encouraging to see first-hand a vision start to become reality. The first customer for your new business, the first neighbor who comes to faith, the first purchase of a property for your family, business, or the church God's called you to plant—this is the fruit of your work and the answer to your prayers, and it is worth celebrating.

During an advancement stage, there are few things to remember. First, this is a stage of hard work. Advancement requires overcoming inertia, solving problems, making decisions, and putting in a lot of hours of work. God will give you the vision and the resources you need, but he won't drag you to the goal while you remain passive. Expect to work, and work hard.

Second, don't let arrogance get a foothold. If you have success in any endeavor, people will praise you. There will be a temptation to take the credit, bask in the glory, and begin to think you know more than you do. There is no quicker route to the destruction of what you have built than letting pride enter your heart. The Bible and world history— including, sadly, the history of the church in some cases—demonstrate all too clearly the power of pride to bring ruin. Stay humble, stay teachable, stay grateful. God has given you success, and only he can sustain you. Centuries after Abraham's death, when his descendants finally took possession of the land promised to them, Moses gave them advice that is still relevant today: "But remember the Lord your God, for it is he who gives you the ability to produce wealth, and so confirms his covenant, which he swore to your ancestors, as it is today" (Deuteronomy 8:18).

Finally, pay attention to balance and boundaries. Stages of advancement are busy, and the urgency of the work can be compelling. God isn't asking you to burn out mentally, emotionally, physically, or spiritually for the sake of the call. If you find yourself saying to an exhausted spouse or a worried mentor, "I know we're busy, but it's just a season," stop and ask yourself how often you say that. An exhausting two weeks of work is one thing. An exhausting year or decade is quite another. Find rhythms, even in stages of advancement, that make life doable for you and your family. Romans 14:17 says that the kingdom of

God is "righteousness, peace, and joy in the Holy Spirit." Is your household marked by those three things, or have you allowed the pressures of your responsibilities or your ambition to be replaced by corner-cutting, stress, and anxiety? Jesus said his yoke is easy and his burden light (Matthew 11:30). If your burden feels impossibly heavy, get alone with God and ask him to reveal what needs to change.

Testing and Pruning Stages

Abraham soon ran into a problem, and it was a big one: famine. Unlike earlier, when things were going well, this time Abraham didn't build an altar to God. As far as we know, he didn't ask God for help or wait to see if God would provide. Instead, he fled with his family to Egypt. There, he became scared that someone would kill him in order to take his wife Sarah for himself, so he passed her off as his sister. Eventually, Pharaoh himself took Sarah into his palace with the intention of making her his wife. God intervened by sending plagues on the Egyptians until they gave Sarah back and kicked the whole family out of Egypt (Genesis 12:10–20).

Later on, he faced other trials, including years of childlessness and then a challenge to give up the son that finally was born as a sacrifice to God (in case you're not familiar with that story, God didn't actually have him kill his son). The call was tested over and over again. In some cases, Abraham responded with amazing faith and trust. In other cases, such as the fiasco in Egypt, he didn't respond well at all. But in every case, God guided him through the tests and used those stages to strengthen and purify Abraham.

Testing, trials, and barriers are such an important part of our response to God's call that they are the subject of the entire next chapter. But for now, just be aware that testing stages will happen repeatedly in our lives. And while we'd rather spend all our time advancing and little or no time being tested, both are important stages in our journey. Together, they help us move forward in ways that are healthy and God-honoring.

Altars

One of the most significant parts of Abraham's story to me is not technically a stage at all, although it is related to key stages. Time and again on his journey, Abraham stopped to build an altar.

After arriving in Shechem in Canaan (the conclusion of a significant advancement stage), God appeared to him and promised that the land would someday belong to his descendants. Abraham responded by building an altar and worshiping (Genesis 12:6–7). Then he moved on to Bethel, where he also built an altar and called on the name of the Lord (verse 8). After his detour to Egypt and subsequent return to Bethel, Abraham again called on the name of the Lord, most likely at that same altar (13:3–4). He went on to do the same several more times in his life.

Altars were significant not just in Abraham's life but throughout Scripture. The word is used four hundred times in the Old Testament alone. It meant more than just a pile of rocks or a piece of furniture in the temple that Abraham's descendants would one day build. An altar was a place of sacrifice, worship, and covenant relationship with God. It was a place where heaven and earth touched. At key moments in Abraham's life, he made sure his focus was on God and that he was aligned with God's purposes.

I've never built a literal altar or sacrificed an animal as a means of worship (I can only imagine what my HOA would say if I did.) We don't have to offer sacrifices because Jesus already offered himself once and for all for our sins.

The concept of the altar is still integral to our faith journey, though. The principle of stopping to spend time with God, focusing intentionally on his purposes and our covenant relationship with him, is something we must practice regularly, We live each day with both the culture around us and our own sin nature pulling us away from God's purposes and trying to conform us to the ways of sinful humanity. If we are to remain aligned with God's purposes, we need a consistent pattern of altar building.

"Alignment" is the proper positioning of parts in relation to each other. It is a movement intended to bring something into a place of maximum efficacy, strength, and safety by positioning it in the correct relationship to the other parts in a system.

Alignment with God happens through altar building. It happens when I intentionally set aside time to focus on God for the same reasons that Abraham did:

> To thank God for taking care of me and my family.
>
> To remind myself that I have committed my way to God and that he has promised to bless me and lead me.
>
> To spend unhurried time in the presence of God, listening for what he might want to say.
>
> To give something of value—my time and attention—to God because I deeply value my relationship with him.
>
> To make a public declaration that I will serve the living God and I will obey his words to me.

When we do this, our priorities and perspectives come back into alignment with God. Altar-centered worship admits our need, reaffirms our surrender to God, encourages the growth of humility, keeps us from presumptive living, and helps us remove idols that have crept into our lives without us noticing.

The outcome of a consistent, altar-centered worship life is yielding to God on his terms. When we are in this state, every stage we go through becomes filled with God's power and directed toward his purposes. Whether we are just starting our journey, experiencing success, or going through a time of pain and trial, alignment with God through altar building helps us stay on the path.

For me, altar building is my daily time of prayer with God, along with an annual rhythm that includes two prayer retreats where I go away alone just to read, pray, and listen. It also involves times of fasting, as well as corporate prayer and worship with other believers, both in small groups and churchwide. When I pray it isn't to impress God or complete a checklist. It's an intentional time of surrender and posturing myself to best hear God.

If you want to thrive in every stage, even the most challenging ones, I challenge you to make altar building central to your life. Set aside time each day to be in the presence of God, consciously surrendering to him and acknowledging his sovereignty. Align yourself with his purposes and learn to hear his still, small voice.

We need this in every stage, although we don't always recognize it when things are going well. But God is very faithful to remind us of our need for him by giving us a priceless gift most of us would prefer to avoid trials. That's the topic we turn to next.

Questions for Reflection

1. What is a major move you have made in response to God's prompting? Did you experience immediate advancement or was the first stage something else?

2. Think of a time when you experienced testing and trials while obeying God. What was most difficult about that time? What did you learn?

3. "Building altars" in this chapter refers to intentionally spending time with God to realign your priorities with his. What are some ways you build altars? How does it affect your thinking and your actions?

Chapter 11

THE CONFLICT

N o movement lasts long without running into difficulties. For Abraham, as I mentioned in the last chapter, it was a famine that stopped him in his tracks. That must have been bewildering to him: God had promised not just to provide for his family but to bless them extravagantly. Yet responding to God's call had led them right into a crisis. A famine could easily ruin them financially; it could even become a matter of life and death if it persisted.

Abraham didn't handle that test well, to be honest. But before we judge him too harshly, what do we do when faced with crises? We might not have to deal with a literal famine, but we will absolutely face challenges of similar intensity as we respond to God's call. We will find ourselves in difficult situations that are outside of our control. We will be tempted to run, to quit, to compromise our integrity in order to make a way of escape for ourselves. It is in those moments that God reveals things in our hearts, both good and bad, that we would not otherwise see. And he does so in order to help us on our journey.

Stages of testing and trial are not fun times. They are miserable and sometimes even traumatic, and Satan would love to use them to shipwreck our faith entirely. But God has a different purpose.

If we handle them right, stages of challenge and trial become catalysts to bring us closer to God and teach us invaluable truths that will further us on our journey. If we enter into these stages with the right knowledge and heart attitude, we can position ourselves to learn from them rather than being destroyed by them.

Entire books have been written on the topic of suffering, and you and I both have a few chapters of our own we could write. We've all suffered. We've faced barriers, tasted defeat, born the burden of discouragement. No one is immune from setbacks, no matter how faith-filled, wise, or holy.

Jesus himself faced trials of all kinds, and he promised we would, too. After his resurrection, he told his disciples, "I have told you these things, so that in me you may have peace. In this world you will have trouble. But take heart! I have overcome the world" (John 16:33).

If I'm honest, part of me would prefer to have the second half of that verse without the first half. I'm a big fan of Jesus overcoming the world. I'm not such a big fan of having trouble. But the longer I walk with Jesus, the more I understand and even value the times of suffering and setbacks. Some of my most intimate moments in the presence of God have come during times of brokenness. My relationship with Michal and my kids has grown stronger as we've walked shoulder to shoulder through chaos. My faith has been strengthened, my calling confirmed, and my perspective enlarged by times of testing.

> But God is able to use those same crises to bring us into a place of hope, peace, and faith that no storm can destroy.

But while these things are easy to believe when things are going well, they are much harder to affirm in the maelstrom of a crisis. When my daughter was first diagnosed with a brain tumor, I didn't start rejoicing. I didn't immediately thank God for the opportunity to have my faith stretched. I reacted as any father would: grief, fear, anger, denial, bargaining with God, and frantic attempts to find a way out of a reality I hadn't planned for and wouldn't have wished on anyone.

By God's grace and through a stubborn belief in the Word of God, our family was able to choose to trust God in that storm. We weathered it without being shipwrecked in our faith. But it was often messy, sometimes overwhelming, and never easy.

I don't know where you're at in your journey. I do know that neither you nor I have endured our last storm. We will face times of crisis that threaten to shipwreck us. But God is able to use those same crises to bring us into a place of hope, peace, and faith that no storm can destroy.

Every movement initiated by God, whether in our personal life or the corporate life of his church, will face trials. How we respond to them will shape the next stages of our journey.

No Greater Faithfulness

Quite possibly the greatest truth I've experienced in the trials I've been through is this: God is more patient and loving with us than we could ever imagine. Abraham didn't handle his first test well (although he did better in some later ones). In his panic, he was willing to put his wife at risk of being married to Pharaoh to save his own skin. But God was faithful and patient even in Abraham's weakness. He protected the family and provided a means of escape. He didn't give up on Abraham the first time Abraham's faith wavered. There is no greater faithfulness than the faithfulness of God toward his people.

Some Christians I talk with are afraid that God is mad at them, or at least running out of patience with them. They see their mistakes and their problems and wonder how God could use them. They fear being rejected or punished if they fail at anything. Sometimes, they realize this tendency about themselves (which is good, actually, as awareness is often the first step toward change), while other times, the fear is more subconscious. They try all kinds of coping mechanisms to resolve the guilt: developing a compulsion to be perfect, blame shifting or making excuses, cutting others down to make themselves feel better, becoming defensive when confronted or criticized, or avoiding challenges to minimize the potential shame of failure.

Those coping tactics don't really work, and they often hurt others around them. I actually think we'd struggle a lot less with perfectionism, defensiveness, blame-shifting, and avoidance if we had a better understanding of God's incredible love and patience toward us. It's not that the Bible isn't clear about it. Romans 8:31-39 says this:

> What, then, shall we say in response to these things? If God is for us, who can be against us? He who did not spare his own Son, but gave him up for us all—how will he not also, along with him, graciously give us all things? Who will bring any charge against those whom God has chosen? It is God who justifies. Who then is the one who condemns? No one. Christ Jesus who died—more than that, who was raised to life—is at the right hand of God and is also interceding for us. Who shall separate us from the love of Christ? Shall trouble or hardship or persecution or famine or nakedness or danger or sword? As it is written:
> "For your sake we face death all day long;
> we are considered as sheep to be slaughtered."
> No, in all these things we are more than conquerors through him who loved us. For I am convinced that neither death nor life, neither angels nor demons, neither the present nor the future, nor any powers, neither height nor depth, nor anything else in all creation, will be able to separate us from the love of God that is in Christ Jesus our Lord.

Those are life-changing words to anyone buried under condemnation or an unhealthy fear of God. Nothing can separate us from God's love! There is no one left to condemn us! God himself justifies us (that means he declares us to be righteous) based on Jesus' death for us. There is probably no truth in the Bible more encouraging to us when we are struggling than this. *God is on our side, so who can be against us?*

If we start to think our own weaknesses might somehow disqualify us from this love, the Bible has plenty of examples of people who failed spectacularly and yet were still loved and used by God. Samson,

Moses, David, Jonah, Peter, and scores of others all found out firsthand just how extravagant the grace and mercy of God are.

You and I serve that same God, and his mercies are still new every morning. So if you don't respond perfectly in a time of trial or testing, don't lose hope. The adversary of your soul wants to discourage you, but God is ready to lift you up and bring you to victory.

This doesn't mean there won't be consequences for poor decisions. We live in a real world with real consequences, and sometimes the price for our mistakes is steep. But even when we are facing the pain that comes from our poor choices or the choices of others, God isn't about to give up on us. And he is more than able to use the pain—even the pain we bring on ourselves—to move us along on our journey.

The Fire of Purification

Another thing about testing stages that is crucial to understand is their value in purifying us. Fire both reveals and burns away impurities. Abraham's faith and trust in God had a limit, and famine revealed that. Countless times, I've said, thought, prayed, and sung songs about my trust in God. But when a crisis hits, my internal and external responses reveal how much of that trust was genuine and how much was just naive self-deception.

Hebrews 12 tells us to look at trials as discipline. It assures us that every one of us will undergo discipline because God has made us his children and cares enough to help us grow. It reminds us that discipline never feels pleasant at the time, but that the pain actually has a vital purpose, producing "a harvest of righteousness and peace for those who have been trained by it" (verse 11). There are heart attitudes, character deficiencies, and unhealed past hurts that will damage or even destroy us if they are not dealt with. God, in his faithfulness, often uses painful times of testing to bring awareness and correction to those unhealthy areas.

If you're in this fire right now, you know how humbling it is. And that's a good thing. Humility is the posture of purification. Nothing blinds us to our own issues faster than pride and nothing brings healing faster than a heart that is humble—even broken—before God. David, when confronted with the rot in his own heart that had led him to commit horrific sins, responded with humility and brokenness. In that season of grief and shame, he penned these words: "My sacrifice, O God, is a broken spirit; a broken and contrite heart you, God, will not despise" (Psalm 51:17).

God is faithful. He loves you and me more than we could possibly comprehend. And though the fire of purification feels like it is burning us up, it is in reality only burning away what would otherwise destroy us. So, in your pain, respond with humility and trust. Then watch as God brings you through the fire. And like Daniel's friends who were thrown into a fiery furnace for their faith, you will find that the only things that were burned were the ropes that bound you.

Pain Is an Excellent Teacher

Part of the purification process is learning to believe and hold fast to the truth. Pain teaches us things we'd never learn (or at least never learn to obey) in any other way. Experience is a powerful teacher, and painful experiences often teach us the most. In part, that's because trials tend to humble us, and humility is an essential prerequisite for gaining wisdom (Proverbs 11:2). It's also because pain indelibly imprints its lesson on our minds in a way that academic study doesn't. And it's because even though we may understand a truth accurately in an intellectual sense, we often don't grasp the full weight of it until we have a personal experience with it.

Tests reveal truths about God's nature, including his love, faithfulness, holiness, and wisdom. They show us our own needs—the weaknesses or unguarded strengths in us that we had not realized were vulnerable to attack. They help us learn to hear God's voice more clearly, as our desperation motivates us to focus on him in a way that we often neglect during seasons when we feel successful. And in the end, those tests become testimonies of God's faithfulness and power in our lives. They build our faith so that we are ready to face future trials and future successes in a healthier way, and they give us a story that we can share with others to help them in their own times of suffering.

So, the next time you face a trial, ask God to start showing you what he wants you to learn through it. (Maybe even start a list, because you'll find that God often works on more than one thing at a time.) Then hold on, clinging to faith even though the waves of pain and fear seem overwhelming. Know that as you hold on to faith in God, he is holding on to you with arms far stronger than yours will ever be. He is faithful, and he will bring you through.

It's Your Choice

We humans have a complicated relationship with difficulties. On the one hand, we like things to be easy, quick, and convenient. I'm sure I'm not the only one who has grumbled when my coffee order took longer than two minutes to be ready, when an unreasonable number of red lights delayed my commute, or when the driver ahead of me insisted on driving precisely the speed limit in the left lane of the freeway (don't they know that lane is for *crime*?).

On the other hand, we often deliberately seek out challenges. We set goals for ourselves, learn new skills for fun, play online games that test our intellect, or push ourselves to exhaustion playing a favorite sport. (My mountain-climbing friend tells the story of stopping to rest at the halfway point of a climb sometime well before dawn, with the temperature below freezing and a strong wind blowing. As he and his friends huddled in the snow, complaining about the cold, he said, "But if you don't question your life choices at least once…" and someone immediately replied cheerfully, "...is it even a climb?" Everyone chuckled and nodded in agreement, then they slung their packs on their backs and kept climbing.)

So why do we avoid some difficulties and revel in others? Much of it comes down to one word: choice. When we choose a difficult path, it's a challenge. When we get forced onto that path, it's a trial. Same level of difficulty, same amount of suffering, very different perspective.

Maybe that's why Jesus and the writers of the New Testament often frame difficulties as a choice rather than a disaster. Jesus tells us to pick up our cross and follow him (Matthew 16:24). The writer of Hebrews introduces the concept of God using hard times as a means of loving discipline by comparing us to athletes who are running a race and encourages us to make a choice both in how we view trials and in how we respond to them (Hebrews 12:1–13). That same writer tells his readers, who were facing ostracism and social disgrace as a result of their faith, to "go to [Jesus] outside the camp, bearing the disgrace he bore" (13:13), thus helping them see themselves not as victims but as willing participants in Jesus' life and destiny.

In literature, the archetypes of victim and hero share key similarities. Both suffer unfairly. Both face tremendous pain. But one becomes defined by that pain, while the other perseveres through it to attain their goal.

Hard times will come either way, but we get to decide how we will face them.

So what role do we play in our story—victim or hero? Hard times will come either way, but we get to decide how we will face them. Seeing trials as a logical and even necessary outcome of the choice we've made to obey God can help us avoid becoming paralyzed and demoralized by a victim mentality.

Hebrews 11, the famous "Hall of Faith" in Scripture, lists dozens of biblical heroes who performed miracles, overcame difficulties, endured persecution, and stayed faithful to the end. In chapter 12, verse 1, the writer concludes by saying, "Therefore, since we are surrounded by such a great cloud of witnesses, let us throw off everything that hinders and the sin that so easily entangles, and let us run with perseverance the race marked out for us."

God is still looking for heroes today. And he's looking squarely at you and me.

Questions for Reflection

1. Think about a time when you experienced a season of pain, suffering, or trial. How did God meet you in that space? In what ways did you see his love and faithfulness in your pain?

2. During that season of pain, what lessons did you learn?

3. Have you ever chosen to do something even though it was difficult or even painful? How did the fact that you chose it, rather than having it forced on you, change your perspective? How could you reframe the trials you are experiencing right now to see your role as a hero rather than a victim?

Chapter 12

THE COMMUNITY

E arlier, we discussed the importance of three types of relation-ships: *up* (God), *in* (our family, church, friends), and *out* (our neighbors, the world). I included that toward the beginning of this book for a reason: relationships aren't optional. They are core to understanding, experiencing, and sharing the gospel, and they are an integral part of the journey you are on.

God's call on your life is big. In fact, it's almost certainly bigger than you even know right now. As you move forward in response to his call, he will open door after door, leading you into a future full of promise and hope.

But you won't do that alone. Our journey isn't a solo quest. God's full purpose in our lives is always accomplished in and through com-munity: families, teams, business partners, and the local church.

When Abraham obeyed God, he was joined by his wife Sarah, his nephew Lot, numerous household servants, and eventually, chil-dren of his own. As God blessed him, his community grew—a lot. Sometimes, we imagine them as a single tiny family plodding through the desert from oasis to oasis with a couple of servants to help. But Genesis 14 tells the fascinating story of what happened when Lot and some others were kidnapped by an alliance of four kings and their armies. Abraham went after them, along with 318 trained men who were part of his household, and rescued everyone who had been taken. To have a personal army of over three hundred men means his "household" probably included several thousand people.[11] Abraham wasn't just the head of a family; he was the ruler of a tribe powerful enough to conquer regional kings.

I don't know about your household, but mine certainly doesn't have its own army (although it feels like I'm feeding one sometimes). But the principle is still the same. God brings people around us to help us fulfill the vision he has birthed in our spirits.

That means God's promises on my life involve all those in my sphere—my spouse, children, local church, and others whose lives intersect with mine. My story is a thread, but God is weaving a tapestry. My thread strengthens yours, and yours strengthens mine. Together we become a work of divine art, a masterpiece for his glory, a living testimony of God's power and love.

Regardless of what God has placed in your heart to do or to become, other people will play a key role in bringing that to reality, and you will play a role in their destiny as well. That's the beauty of life in God's kingdom and as a part of his movement. We get to partner with other people, helping one another along on our journeys. We are all in this together.

Life at the Table

Life at the table isn't a church growth strategy at our church. It's part of our identity. It's who we are. I wrote an entire chapter on it earlier in this book, but the idea is so countercultural in our individualistic and results-driven culture that it needs to be brought to the forefront regularly or we'll fall back into our old ways of thinking.

The table is a place of nourishment, fellowship, sharing, and hospitality. It is where we listen to one another, where our hearts are bonded in unity, where ideas are formed and shaped and launched into reality, and where God brings individuals together into destiny-shaping relationships.

We need to continually come back to the table, for our own sakes and for those whom God is calling us to influence. It may feel easier at times to go it alone because relationships are complicated, and sometimes it just seems simpler and less painful to keep our distance from others.

But God didn't create us to live solitary lives. Our faith is meant to be lived out in community. When Jesus taught his disciples, he did it by forming a small community. His teachings were often not sermons or lectures; they were responses to conflicts or questions that came up as that small group followed him, sharing a table and a dream.

When Jesus taught them to pray, he began with, "Our Father in heaven." You can't even get past the first word of the Lord's Prayer without confronting the reality that he's not just my Father. He's our Father.

There is a richness and joy in the context of a healthy community that can be found nowhere else. Yes, it's challenging. And yes, the vulnerability of opening ourselves up to others includes the risk of being hurt. Loving and being loved in a broken world are not simple. But they are beautiful.

Author and theologian C.S. Lewis, in his book The Four Loves, describes the risks and the blessings of love this way:

> To love at all is to be vulnerable. Love anything, and your heart will certainly be wrung and possibly be broken. If you want to make sure of keeping it intact, you must give your heart to no one, not even to an animal. Wrap it carefully round with hobbies and little luxuries; avoid all entanglements; lock it up safe in the casket or coffin of your selfishness. But in that casket—safe, dark, motionless, airless—it will change. It will not be broken; it will become unbreakable, impenetrable, irredeemable. The alternative to tragedy, or at least to the risk of tragedy, is damnation. The only place outside Heaven where you can be perfectly safe from all the dangers and perturbations of love is Hell.[12]

I've been hurt by letting others into my life, and you probably have, too. But that can't cause us to pull back from relationships. There is richness, joy, strength, and peace in life at the table with the community of God that we desperately need.

God is calling you to move, but he isn't asking you to do it alone. He has put others in your sphere, people whom he'll use to encourage you, mentor you, challenge you, love you unconditionally, and help you as you pursue God.

He will be faithful to do that your whole life. Some people will be lifelong companions, whether they are family or dear friends. Others will walk with you for one or more stages of your life, and then your paths will diverge. Some will come in and out of your life at unexpected times, bringing blessings and strength when you most need them. Some of these people you know already, and even as you read this, you can see the ways they have helped you. Others you have probably not even met yet, but God is leading them, and you, toward the place where your journeys will intersect.

We Need Help

During the darkest days of our daughter's battle with cancer, something unexpected happened: I fell in love with the church again.

Don't get me wrong, I hadn't rejected the church. My doctrine was intact and I loved the people I was serving. I felt the anointing of the Holy Spirit and enjoyed gathering with believers. But, budgets, leadership responsibilities, vision-casting, decision-making, and problem-solving consumed most of my time. I think if I'm honest, my soul had begun to get just a bit numb to the simple, precious beauty of the life of Jesus among his people. Church had become a place to give, not a place to receive.

Then Mariah was diagnosed with a brain tumor. As soon as we shared the news with the church, we were inundated with messages of caring support, with faith-filled prayers, and with offers of practical help. We felt loved in a way I cannot put into words as people all over the world reached out to strengthen us in our time of crisis.

I remember one experience in particular. The best way to describe what we were experiencing is from Psalm 23, "the valley of the shadow of death." Mariah had just had her first surgery, gone through chemotherapy and radiation, and was literally learning to walk again. I remember having to help her up and down the stairs and support her as she tripped over her own feet. My own heart was broken as I witnessed and shared in her pain.

Just when we were hopeful we would get a good report, she had a seizure while sitting in a college lecture. The campus where she was a student is up the hill from my office, so I ran there, barely beating the ambulance. When I arrived, I found her leaning up against the corner of the room, completely unresponsive to my pleas. Another scan revealed the tumor had grown back, and this time it was even larger than before. She needed another surgery, one the doctor warned us she might not survive.

I cried myself to sleep that night, and I think my wife did the same. The next morning, I remember thinking, *Just getting out of bed is going to take all the faith I've got today.* I felt guilty for not having more boldness, but at that moment, I was just too broken and too spent.

I pushed myself off the mattress and picked my phone up from the bedside table. There were several messages there from a friend I'd gone to college with decades before. When I opened them, I saw a series of videos he'd sent in the middle of the night. Because of the time difference, while we were sleeping, he had been recording videos of his family gathered at a table singing, praying, and declaring victory over my family, and especially my daughter.

I've always believed and taught that every member of Christ's body has an active role to play. Mostly though, I'd thought of this in terms of people's ministry gifts. I'd valued the growth and forward movement of the church that comes when God's people join their talents and skills to achieve a common vision.

But that morning, I experienced the body of Christ in a whole new dimension. God poured out his love on our hurting family through his people in a way that created awe, hope, joy, and a deep and abiding trust. In a moment when my hope was crushed and my faith level so low that just getting out of bed in the morning used it all up, someone else was praying on our behalf. Intercession did rise like incense. It just didn't come from me. Someone else was praying on our behalf.

That day, the numbness that had unknowingly crept into my soul toward the church went away. Now I see a spiritual family, woven together in love and mighty in God. Each one is filled with the Spirit. Each one stands ready to love and support another in need, even if they are halfway around the world in the middle of the night.

Yes, we need the spiritual gifts that each member brings to the body—wisdom, faith, discernment, prophetic words, administration, leadership, and a host of other gifts the Spirit has distributed throughout the body. They make us more effective as a team and help advance the movement of Jesus. That's wonderful and valuable.

But if we look at the church as just a group of people with useful skills, we miss the richness of being part of God's family. Achieving goals together isn't fundamentally what defines a family, even if we do accomplish a lot more working together than alone. When focused only on goals, the church is transactional and people feel used. At its heart, family is about unconditional commitment and steadfast love. It's a tapestry of diverse peoples, woven together with honor and esteem, creating something far more beautiful than any

> We're part of a powerful family, empowered by the Spirit of God, and we're never alone.

one single part could ever be or do on their own. In this way, when one member suffers, the others feel that pain, and when a member rejoices, the others join in the celebration (1 Corinthians 12:26).

What's in the middle of it all is the blood of Jesus, pulsating through our lives. He's the vine we're meant to abide in. And when we do, we're part of a powerful family, empowered by the Spirit of God, and we're never alone. There's an eternal cloud of witnesses cheering us on. A local body who can bring meals and care deeply for us. And a movement of saints across the earth who are activated by the Spirit to stand in the gap for us when we don't have strength to stand.

God's Spirit and Us

As an American, the culture I see around me celebrates self. Self-help, self-empowerment, self-love, self-care...the list goes on. There are aspects of this that are healthy. We are made in God's image. We have value, we are loved by God, and we have legitimate needs that should be met. But when the pendulum of self-worth swings so far that we focus only on ourselves and deny our need for others, we cut ourselves off from the richness of true community.

Think about one of the most famous lists in the Bible: the "fruit of the Spirit" in Galatians 5:22–23. We often think of these as character qualities that each of us should grow in. We interpret them individually because that's the worldview lens we tend to use when we read Scripture. But every single one of those fruits is primarily—and sometimes exclusively—evident in the context of community. You can't demonstrate love, for example, without someone to receive that love. And you're unlikely to become more patient without a few frustrating people around you to practice on!

In fact, if you read the context of the passage, the list is tied to what it means "to love your neighbor as yourself" (verse 14). The work of the Spirit in our lives is shown most clearly in how we treat one another. It's community-focused, not me-focused.

That fruit of the Holy Spirit—love, joy, peace, patience, kindness, goodness, faithfulness, gentleness, and self-control—transforms our relationships with others, enabling us to be a community that models Jesus to one another and to the world. As we submit to the Holy Spirit's work in us, our lives change.

We begin to *love* others better and learn to receive their love for us. That love is shown in our care and concern for others, our ability to empathize, our willingness to sacrifice for each other, and our steadfast desire to see God's best for each other's lives.

We experience genuine *joy* in our relationships. Our trust in God's power and love enables us to release fear, reach out, celebrate others' successes, and truly enjoy the richness of sharing life's ups and downs with others.

We increasingly experience *peace* in our relationships with others. We learn the humility, repentance, honesty, and courage needed to resolve hurts and overcome the inevitable problems that arise in any relationship, and as we let God's Spirit lead, he brings a supernatural peace that is worth more than any material wealth or success.

All of these fruits of the Spirit's work are revealed and strengthened in the context of community.

We develop *patience* with other people (and with God, as he rarely operates on our timetable). The challenges and frustrations of working together with others help us see where we need to grow, revealing immaturity or buried hurts that God wants to deal with.

We have opportunities to engage in acts of *kindness* toward others, and we benefit from their kindness toward us. Kindness breaks down relational barriers, communicates love, heals wounds, and knits hearts together.

We begin to understand *goodness* in a fresh way. Goodness isn't an action; it's a character quality that radically transforms how we treat others. Our goodness is not why God saves us (we could never be good enough to deserve his love), but rather it is what he does in us.

We develop *faithfulness* in our interactions with others, growing in integrity and dependability. As we become more faithful, trust begins to grow, and our relationships become marked by peace and graciousness rather than suspicion.

We learn the value of *gentleness*. We all carry a burden of pain to some degree, and in those areas where we are hurting, we want to be treated with gentleness, not harshness. Life at the table helps us learn to listen to each other's stories and understand that pain so we can come alongside each other with tenderness and compassion.

Finally, we grow in *self-control*. Relationships aren't easy, and often they stir up difficult emotions: anger, frustration, or fear. Our tendency in those times is to protect ourselves, often by lashing out at others or by acting out in some unhealthy way. But as we grow in the other fruits of the Spirit, we learn to handle those emotions in a healthier way and to control ourselves to avoid hurting others.

All of these fruits of the Spirit's work are revealed and strengthened in the context of community. It's not just me becoming more like Jesus, it's us becoming more like him.

Who has God brought into your life to walk alongside you? Who is speaking into your life, partnering with you, and helping you achieve the vision God has given you? If you can identify a few people, take a moment to thank God for them. They are gifts from a loving Father to enrich and strengthen your life. Then ask him how you can serve them better and how their strengths can fill in the gaps you might have.

Community is challenging and complex, yes. But it is so, so rich. You have much to offer the rest of the body of Christ and much to receive.

Questions for Reflection

1. What does the phrase "life at the table" mean to you? How could living this way bless others? How could it bless you?

2. Have you ever experienced a time in your life when you needed help from your church family? How did they respond, and how did that impact you?

3. Think about the fruit of the Holy Spirit listed in Galatians: love, joy, peace, patience, kindness, goodness, faithfulness, gentleness, and self-control. Is there one of these in particular that God is emphasizing to you right now? How might he want you to demonstrate or grow in that fruit in the context of your community?

Chapter 13

THE BLESSING

I referred in an earlier chapter to the worship song by Kari Jobe and others called "The Blessing," released by Elevation Church. The lyrics are biblical, from a priestly blessing in Numbers 6:24–26, but the song itself is a bit unconventional. Worship songs are typically either to God or about him. This song, however, is written directly to the church. In simple, powerful language, it calls for God's blessing to be on all believers and our descendants.

"The Blessing" was released in March 2020, the same month that COVID-19 restrictions began to be implemented across the US, and it quickly swept the globe. As church gatherings moved online and many people were confined to their homes, people began collaborating online to produce versions of the song that featured believers from all over the world singing successive lines of the song in their own languages. People who had never met one another declared God's goodness, love, and power in the face of a worldwide crisis. There was something indescribably powerful and faith-building about singing those words in the midst of that storm. Despite all the pain our world was experiencing, we were declaring together that God's purposes in our lives were still good and his power was still supreme. "The Blessing" became an anthem of hope and faith for a global church determined to keep believing for God's blessing to be fulfilled.

The concept of blessing is as ancient as human history. The first thing God did after creating humanity was bless us (Genesis 1:28). What a powerful, prophetic indicator of God's heart toward us. The first voice Adam heard was God's, and the first words were words of blessing!

Because the word blessed is a common term used in Christianity, most people believe they know what it means, so when it is read, it's often passed over, and its depth of meaning is missed. Blessing is something that God initiated and was first in order before human-kind's calling, purpose, or delegated sphere of authority was given. Anything with this level of preeminence should be viewed with utmost importance.

> God longs to open the windows of heaven and bless us with all the richness that a loving Father can give to the children he loves.

What we learn from the first mention of the word is that blessing was foundational to humanity's identity and purpose. At its core, blessing was God the Father's identity, sense of value, and heart of love, declared and imparted over his creation. It was a statement of identity, affirmation, favor, promise, and inheritance. Blessing would build into the human race the confident assurance that who they were and all they would undertake would carry significance because it flowed from a position of the Father's blessing. They could be secure because they were loved and blessed by their Father.

God's character hasn't changed, nor has his love for those he created. Every genre of Scripture—from the stories and prophecies of the Old Testament to Jesus' parables in the Gospels to the apostles' teachings in the Epistles to the end-times visions of Revelation—shouts the same truth: God longs to open the windows of heaven and bless us with all the richness that a loving Father can give to the children he loves.

Sometimes that concept has been twisted into a self-centered, "God is a genie who grants my wishes" version of Christianity. This lie reduces our loving Father to a heavenly Santa Claus who can be manipulated if we just do the right things or speak the correct words. It's nothing more than magic with a Christian veneer, and discerning Christians rightly reject it.

True Christianity is the way of the cross: death to our selfish desires, surrender to God's plan, and a willingness to suffer for the sake of Christ. But in our desire to stay true to this message of the cross, we cannot forget the reason for it. Jesus died to redeem us, set us free, bring us into God's family, make us holy, give us peace and joy and hope and purpose, set us in a loving community, heal us, bless our families and our finances, and give us eternal life. If that's not blessing, I don't know what is!

I believe God wants to bless us far beyond anything we can ask or think. I believe his calling on our lives is not only meant to accomplish his purposes and advance his movement, but it is also to unlock the windows of heaven and drench us with his blessings.

We see that intention in God's call to Abraham. The words "bless" and "blessing" are used four times in two verses:

> I will make you into a great nation,
>   and I will bless you;
> I will make your name great,
>   and you will be a blessing.
> I will bless those who bless you,
>   and whoever curses you I will curse;
> and all peoples on earth
>   will be blessed through you.
> (Genesis 12:2–3)

Each of these statements reveals something about God's desire to bless his creation.

I Will Bless You

God initiated his covenant of blessing with Abraham. Abraham didn't come before God with a list of demands, twisting God's arm to give him what he wanted. God reached out and chose him. God also dictated the type of blessing. Abraham's part was to believe and obey.

God has done the same for you and me. He chose us before the foundation of the earth (Ephesians 1:4). He gave us each gifts and abilities, ones he chose for us rather than ones we picked for ourselves (1 Corinthians 12:4–11). He created us to do good works that he ordained before we were even born (Ephesians 2:10).

We have been given blessings we don't deserve, gifts we didn't ask for, and destiny beyond anything we could imagine. Our part is to believe and obey. In doing that, we will be blessed.

If God is the initiator, then we have a responsibility to listen to his voice so that we can partner with him. That's one reason that daily times of prayer are so important. If we are in tune with his Spirit, then our words and actions are empowered by him, and his blessings are poured out in and through us.

That helps us avoid the "God is Santa Claus" heresy I mentioned earlier. We don't come to God demanding our way like spoiled brats. Instead, we have a posture of bold humility, listening for God to speak and then responding in courageous confidence to what he says. When we come before the throne of God to ask for things, we do so boldly (Hebrews 4:16) because we are asking him to do what he's already promised he would do.

The beautiful thing about this is that what God initiates, he also empowers. Our response to God's call isn't about us frantically trying to marshal the resources, connections, and energy to successfully do what God has told us to do. It's about partnering with the God of unlimited resources and letting him bring about the fulfillment of his word. It is so easy for us to fall into the trap of thinking that God's promises are up to us to fulfill and that somehow the vision he's dropped into our heart is our job to accomplish. We get a sense of what he wants to do through us and immediately feel an overwhelming sense of responsibility to make sure it happens.

But as much as we like to think that we have a handle on things, we don't have the ability to control our future. No matter how good our planning skills might be, our knowledge cannot account for all contingencies. And regardless of how hard we work to ensure our motives are pure, our own fallen natures (not to mention those of people around us) intervene to trip us up.

The simple fact is our success does not depend nearly as much on us as our ego would like to think. That's actually good news for believers, though, because it's in our very weakness that God's strength is revealed (2 Corinthians 12:9). It's when a crisis overwhelms my coping skills or a problem becomes too complicated for me to plan my way out of that I'm most aware of God's power in my life. He has decreed blessing over my life and yours, and he will be faithful to bring it to pass.

Of course, we have a responsibility as well. The premise of this book is that God is calling his people to move in response to his call on our lives. But simple obedience based in faith is all he's asking for from us. The rest is his job.

You Will Be a Blessing

Immediately after telling Abraham his plans to bless him, God followed it with, "and you will be a blessing." God's blessing is never just for us. It's so that we can be a blessing to those in our sphere too.

We actually understand this principle instinctively. When I was a young church planter, there were times when people blessed me unexpectedly with a financial gift. Never once did I immediately make plans to spend it all on myself. My response was always to use it to bless my family. And often, Michal and I would set aside a portion of that gift to bless someone else in need. That didn't require me to grit my teeth and force myself to "do the right thing." It was instinctive. When we receive blessings, it's the most natural thing in the world to want to turn around and share them with others.

The list of gifts God has given us is staggering, if we take the time to think about them. Life itself is a gift. The beauty of a sunrise is a gift. Relationships, joy, play, rest, health, energy, and love are all gifts. And when we come into God's family, he gives us eternal life, freedom from addictions, peace, purpose, forgiveness, his Holy Spirit, better relationships, wisdom, and a thousand other priceless blessings.

But he didn't give us all those things so we could hoard them for ourselves. They are meant to be shared. And in God's economy, what we give away just makes us richer. Sharing his blessings with others enriches our lives in a way that hoarding them for ourselves could never do. I'm not talking just about money, although it applies to money as well, and we are instructed to share with those in need (Hebrews 13:16, Ephesians 4:28). I'm talking about everything. Every gift God gives can be shared in one way or another: your wisdom can guide others, your patience can extend them grace when they need it, your peace can calm their fears, your love can help them feel safe enough to get back up and try again.

> When you enter a room, blessing does too.

God told Abraham that Abraham himself would be a blessing to the world. Blessing is more than what we do. It is the very essence of *who we are* as God's children. Jesus compared us to salt and light in the world (Matthew 5:13–16). Salt doesn't have to do anything to flavor and preserve food—its very essence is transformative. Light doesn't have to do anything either. It simply shows up, and darkness flees. We are the Body of Christ, the tangible expression of God on earth. Blessing is more than what we receive or what we do—it's who we are.

When you enter a room, blessing does too. That's not because of anything you have done and it's certainly not to bring you glory. It's simply because you are God's child and his emissary to the world. God loves each person in that room, and he wants to use you to express it.

What would our lives be like if we embraced this principle wholeheartedly? What if we saw ourselves quite literally as the conduits of God's love to this world? What if every word we spoke was meant to bless others? What if we listened with compassion, spoke on behalf of the mistreated, stretched out our hands to lift up the stumbling, and proclaimed the unfailing mercy of God to the broken people all around us?

I see a church that is called to do exactly this. We are meant to be a blessing to our city and our world. As we receive God's blessing and respond to his voice, we become salt and light everywhere we go.

I Will Bless Those Who Bless You

As if the first two statements weren't enough, God followed up with a third: "I will bless those who bless you, and I will curse those who curse you." We need to understand what God was saying to Abraham here, because God hasn't changed and neither have his promises. We are Abraham's descendants through the lineage of faith (Romans 4), and this promise is being fulfilled in and through us.

The primary way Abraham would have understood this sentence is simple: God's blessing included divine protection. God was allying himself with Abraham. He was saying, "Your friends are my friends and your enemies are my enemies." For a man about to take his household on a journey through the desert to an unknown land inhabited by potentially hostile forces, this would have been greatly reassuring.

That need for protection hasn't diminished since Abraham's day. A recent survey found that over half of Americans feel they're in imminent danger at least once a day. Among those aged 25–34, that figure climbed to 75 percent who felt unsafe.[13] And that survey just asked about the danger of being victims of a crime; it didn't include the risk of accidents, illnesses, natural disasters, or financial insecurity. Despite all the "development" of the human race over the past millennia, life is risky, and we all know it.

That is why God's promise is so powerful. We, like Abraham, face situations outside of our control. We are walking through a world that is undeniably dangerous, and no matter how careful we are, we cannot anticipate or counter every risk on our own. But we don't have to. God is our ally. He is on our side. He has promised to care for us, walk beside us, and be our shield and our defender. As Psalm 91 says, "He is my refuge and my fortress, my God, in whom I trust" (verse 2).

That does not mean we will never face trials, challenges, and even tragedies. God's protection isn't a bubble around us that keeps all hard times away. A theology that denies the suffering of believers (or blames tragedies on a lack of faith) is incompatible with the Word of God. Jesus himself suffered, and he promised we would have troubles in this world. Paul spoke bluntly about the sufferings he endured and the toll they took on his mental and emotional health (2 Corinthians 4:8–12; 11:23–29).

But God's protection is still real. Nothing happens outside of what he allows, and even in difficult times we can trust him to do what is best and to help us get through the challenges. In fact, God promises to use everything, even the tragedies, for our ultimate good (Romans 8:28).

That can feel impossible to comprehend when we're walking a pathway of tears. I know. I've been there. But walk long enough, and you begin to see that God is truly an ever-present help in times of trouble. He is the good shepherd, guiding us through the valley of the shadow of death. His faithfulness really is incomprehensible, unstoppable, and infallible. He turns weeping into laughter and mourning into joy. At times he stops the storm. At other times he brings peace in the midst of the wind and waves. Either way, we can trust him.

All Peoples on Earth Will Be Blessed through You

The last line of God's promise to Abraham raises the stakes immensely. Up until this point, the promised blessings had been localized. God had promised to bless Abraham, his family, his descendants, and anyone who treated them well.

But in this last line, God goes global. He loves everyone, not just one particular family or nation. And his promised blessing on Abraham is actually the next step in his plan to redeem every single person on earth willing to return to God.

The rest of the Bible describes the fulfillment of this seed promise. Israel, when obeying God, became a beacon attracting others to God (2 Chronicles 9:1–12). Israelite prophets proclaimed the power and holiness of God to the nations and empires of the ancient world. And when Jesus came, the promise reached its fulfillment. As a descendant of Abraham and the promised Messiah, he offered salvation to anyone regardless of nationality, gender, or social status.

> We are part of God's commitment to bless every nation in the world through the gospel of Jesus.

But while that promise began its ultimate fulfillment through Jesus, its power has not ended. You and I carry it forward to this day. We are created and divinely empowered to bless all the nations of the earth.

That's the impetus behind the mighty missions movements that have carried the gospel around the world. It's the reason believers throughout church history have laid down their lives to preach the gospel in foreign lands. It's why our church plants multi-ethnic campuses in our city and sends church planters out to our nation and the world. It's why we go ourselves or send and support others whom God has called to so. I've had the privilege of visiting a few of the countries where our church's missionaries serve, and it never fails to both humble and thrill me. I've seen firsthand the power of the gospel of Jesus Christ transforming not just individuals but communities in cultures as diverse as Uganda, Romania, Laos, Spain, the Caucasus, Sudan, and Cambodia.

We are part of God's commitment to bless every nation in the world through the gospel of Jesus. We are his movement, his story, the fulfillment of his promise.

The word translated "peoples" (or, in some versions, "nations") in this verse literally means clans or families. In a time period where nations were less important than one's own tribe or family grouping, God wanted to raise Abraham's caring capacity from just his own family to every single community on earth. God saw every tribe and family, and God wanted to bless them.

He still does. He cares about every language group. Every social status. Every marginalized community. Every community of friends. Every generation. Every set of individuals who see themselves as having a unique, shared identity. Every neighborhood cluster of homes and pockets of people found in the city or town where you live. God cares so much that he has chosen to bless them by sending them a priceless gift.

You.

You are chosen by God to be that promised blessing. You have a calling that is beyond anything you could accomplish on your own, but one that will come to fruition as you partner with God in obedience. Maybe that calling is to a foreign nation. Maybe it's to the couple next door who both serve as executive leaders in the marketplace. Maybe it's to a marginalized part of your community. Or maybe it's to all of them.

Let me ask you a question: if God spoke to you in a dream tonight and told you that he intends to bless the families of the earth through you, how would you interpret that when you woke up?

> What families, groups, communities, or nations would spring to your mind?
> What segment of our broken society already stirs not just compassion but an urgency to see change?
> What neighbor do you find yourself thinking about and caring about more than you would expect?
> What missionary's vision stirs your faith and makes you want to be a part of bringing it to fruition through your financial support and prayer?

> What age group or demographic do you find yourself crying out to God to meet in a fresh and powerful way?

I'd like to suggest that those thoughts and emotions might not just be your own. They might be the seeds of faith in your spirit, planted there by the Holy Spirit. They might be a hint of the calling of God in your life. They might be part of what God means when he says he will bless all the peoples of the earth through us.

The motto of our church's college, Portland Bible College, is "Made for More." That's not just a catchy tagline; it's a message we passionately believe. The next generation is made for more than just existence, more than just consumerism, more than just living a "normal" self-centered life. They are made to make a difference in this world. They are made to advance Jesus' movement.

So are you and I. We are all made for more. Francis Xavier, legendary missionary to Asia, was known for telling students to "give up their small ambitions and come eastward to preach the gospel of Christ."[14] I believe that spirit ought to be in all of us. We have a calling that supersedes what we see in front of us. Most of us will spend our lives living in our own communities rather than literally moving overseas, but our heart still needs to beat for the nations (including our own).

We get to participate in Jesus' movement, and the part we play may be much, much bigger than we think. Some of the fruit of our obedience will be evident in our lifetimes. We will see individuals helped, churches started and strengthened, God-centered businesses launched, families helped, and marriages healed as we follow him. But the vast majority of the fruit of our lives will happen in future generations. Abraham received a promise, but he saw only the very beginning of its fulfillment. Thousands of years later, you and I are part of the continuing fulfillment of that promise. In the same way, our obedience will have an impact that will echo through generations to come. People we will never meet will be blessed by our obedience.

That's how Jesus' movement works.

Questions for Reflection _____

1. When you hear the phrase, "God wants to bless you," what is your immediate reaction? Do you embrace that or recoil because of some past unhealthy teaching about it? How would you explain the concept to someone?

2. What are some ways you have seen God's blessing in your life? What are some ways you've seen him bless other people through you?

3. Think beyond your immediate community for a moment. What group of people—a nation, an ethnic group, or a marginalized community outside of your own sphere of daily interaction— might God want to bless in some way through you? What is one practical way this week that you could support them?

ADVANCING JESUS' MOVEMENT

All authority in heaven and on earth has been given to me. Therefore go and make disciples of all nations, baptizing them in the name of the Father and of the Son and of the Holy Spirit, and teaching them to obey everything I have commanded you. And surely I am with you always, to the very end of the age.
Matthew 28:18-20

Chapter 14

WHY, HOW, WHAT

I n the first section of this book, we explored the truth that *we were created to move.* You and I are designed by God to respond to his calling on our lives. That's why movement comes so naturally to us. We are hardwired for it.

In the second section, we looked at a model for movement that I call *life at the table.* Movement is meant to be natural and relational, with the rhythms of our daily life infused with God's purpose.

In the third section, we examined the *mechanics of movement.* Using Abraham's life as a template, we explored what it means to respond to God's call in a healthy way.

In each section, we've looked primarily at how our movements affect our own destinies and those of others in our spheres of influence: family, friends, co-workers, and others God brings into our path.

In this last section, I'd like to lift our vision higher. The message of the Bible isn't primarily about me or you, after all. It's about God. He is accomplishing his purposes on earth, and while you and I are integral parts of that, we are just that: parts, not the whole.

Before Jesus returned to heaven after his resurrection, his last words to his disciples were a command to go and make disciples of all nations. The word "nations" means ethnic groups rather than geographically or politically defined areas. Just like the "peoples" of the promise given to Abraham, this word implies that the gospel will bless every single people group around the globe.

The gospel's transformative power was never meant to be limited to the original group of disciples or to the nation of Israel who first received it. Jesus wanted to start a worldwide movement.

The first chapters of the book of Acts suggest that the disciples largely stayed in and around Jerusalem, preaching the gospel to their community. God blessed those efforts, and the church in Jerusalem grew rapidly. But God's vision was bigger than one community and one local church. There was a lost world that needed to hear the good news.

God's heart is for everyone, and ours needs to be as well.

The growth of that church stirred up opposition among the Jewish religious leaders that culminated in the trial and execution of Stephen, the church's first martyr. Acts 8 says: "On that day a great persecution broke out against the church in Jerusalem, and all except the apostles were scattered throughout Judea and Samaria... Those who had been scattered preached the word wherever they went" (8:1, 4). The rest of Acts is a thrilling testimony of what happened next. Persecution didn't stamp out the fire of the gospel; instead, it fanned it into flames that spread like wildfire through the nations. The effect was so dramatic that when disciples began preaching in Thessalonica, located in what is now Greece, the opponents of Christianity complained that these gospel proclaimers "turned the world upside down" (Acts 17:6, ESV).

The spread of the gospel didn't stop there. It has continued for two thousand years, crossing every conceivable boundary and establishing itself in every country in the world. In dramatic contrast to any other religion, Christianity has transcended geographical and cultural expressions to become truly a worldwide faith that is flourishing in every major region of the world.[15]

You are called to move. So am I. So are our families and our local churches. But the ultimate goal isn't just a collection of individuals obeying God's call in lots of individual, unrelated actions. The goal is a movement—Jesus' movement to reconcile the world to God and create a worldwide community of believers who are salt and light wherever they are located.

We need to see ourselves as part of that movement. It's too easy to focus on what's right in front of us. Our needs, opportunities, desires, vision, and plans can seem like the most important thing in the world. But we need to lift our eyes up and see further. God's call to Abraham challenged him to think globally. Jesus' command to his disciples did the same. God's heart is for everyone, and ours needs to be as well.

My ultimate goal in this book isn't to inspire you to move in obedience to God's call. That's just the first step. My ultimate goal is that we together would form a movement of people who know our calling, understand the heart of God, are empowered by his Spirit, and are committed to work in unity to accomplish his purposes. This isn't my idea. It's God's! He's the one who decided to build his church from "every nation, tribe, people, and language" (Revelation 7:9).

In the last section of this book I want to outline how our church, Mannahouse, approaches this concept of advancing Jesus' movement. This isn't the only way to do it. But it's working for us, and I believe that's because it's rooted in the character and the Word of God. If you're a member of our church, you have probably heard this language many times, and I hope this helps you see why we speak the way we do. If you're part of another local church, I hope this gives you a new lens to see your purpose in life through.

The Golden Circle: Why, How, What _____

Author and speaker Simon Sinek uses a concept called the Golden Circle to help businesses better understand why they exist. You'd think this wouldn't be needed. After all, doesn't every company know why they exist? Well, no, actually. A surprising number of companies have lost their sense of identity without even realizing it. At one time, when they were a scrappy, start-up company, they had a clear sense of vision. But over the years, process became more important than purpose. Keeping the company alive mattered more than why the company existed in the first place. Everyone was still working hard, but—beyond the need to make a living—no one could articulate why they were doing what they were doing.

That isn't just true of Fortune 500 companies. It's an issue with any group of individuals who band together around a common vision, including churches. Over time, processes can become routines. Soon routines become rituals. Purpose gets muddled and passion gets lost. A good example would be the seven churches of Asia that God addressed in Revelation 2 and 3. These local congregations started strong with faith, distinction, focus, and a clear sense of identity and purpose. But over time, some of those congregations strayed from their original calling and passion. It happens. God's response was to call them to repentance, recalibration, and a return to the core of why he'd called them in the first place.

A church or other entity without a clear "why" doesn't necessarily stagnate, however. After all, humans are created to move. We gravitate naturally toward vision and goals. So individuals within a drifting church pursue what they are personally passionate about or what catches their attention. And soon, the church without purpose becomes a church with a thousand purposes, each one pushed forward by a member or group in the church with no real idea how their actions fit or don't fit into the mission of the church. Everyone is busy, and good work gets done. But there is so much wasted potential, so many unnecessary conflicts, so much time spent going down rabbit trails that could have been avoided if the church knew its "why."

Simon Sinek's concept of the Golden Circle has been instrumental in helping us articulate God's calling on our church. If you pastor a church, own a business, oversee a department, or have a dream you hope to see become reality, let me suggest you spend some time prayerfully using this tool.

The concept is simple: If you want to be successful, first understand your "why" and then work out from there.

This "why" is at the core of a church's essence and activity. It is the very purpose and reason a church forms in its inception. To articulate or rekindle a church's "why," leaders and teams must be willing to ask some deep questions such as, "Why do we exist?" and "What is our purpose?"

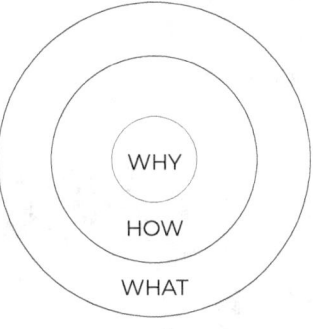

Michal and I, along with some other leaders, began asking those very questions as part of our desire to be faithful to God's call on our church. Going all the way back to humanity's origin, continuing through the Scriptures, and tracing the storyline of Mannahouse from her humble beginnings, it became clear that our "why" is *to advance Jesus' movement*. We were struck by the realization that we have been invited into a story that was in motion before us and will continue long after us. It's all about Jesus, after all. By God's grace and mercy, we've been called to represent his movement in the place where we live.

Given that "why," we next needed to ask, "How will we accomplish it?" As we studied the life and ministry of Jesus, we saw that before he healed a person or preached to crowds, he invited two people to follow him on a lifetime journey of discipleship. Later, he commissioned his disciples by saying, "Go and make disciples of all nations." That directive, found in Matthew 28:18, is the defining framework for "How" a follower of Jesus is meant to advance Jesus' movement—through *disciples making disciples*.

This is a revolutionary idea, not because it's new (it's as old as the gospel) but because it's so foreign to Western culture—and, by extension, so rare in so many churches in our part of the world. Discipleship doesn't happen naturally in our lifestyles, so it is crucial that we intentionally work to develop a culture in our churches where discipleship happens.

Finally, if we are to advance Jesus' movement through disciple-making, we then have to ask, "what should a person experience when they encounter a disciple?" What do we actually do that encourages discipleship and thus advances Jesus' movement? Once again, the Scriptures provide the answer to that question. A recurring theme in Jesus' life and ministry, continued in the early church, was *life at the table*. Again, this doesn't fit naturally into our lifestyles in the way

that it might have in ancient Eastern cultures. But in many ways, that makes it all the more powerful! As we invite people into our lives, discipleship feels organic, natural, and unforced.

Life at the table means more than just going out to eat with friends after a service. A church that does life at the table breaks the bread of God's Word together, shares our lives with one another in vulnerability, and gives away what is in our hand for others. We proclaim the Lord's death until he comes, comforting one another with the ultimate hope we have in the second coming of Christ. This is the culture and the experience people should have when they encounter Jesus' disciples, whether in a corporate gathering, a small group, at events, in homes, or in the marketplace. People should know and experience a movement of disciples who embrace life at the table together.

The Bible is clear that Jesus is building his church, and we are part of that. A key reason we each exist, and a core reason a local church gathers, is to advance Jesus' movement. The way we do that is the way Jesus told us to do it: going into all the world and making disciples through the power of the Holy Spirit. What that looks like on a day-to-day basis is life at the table: hospitality, sharing with others, being vulnerable, advocating for those who need our voice added to theirs, and modeling the love of a God who was willing to leave heaven and do life with us.

We move together, and through our obedience, Jesus changes the world. I can't think of a more exciting reason to live!

Questions for Reflection

1. Think about a group you are a member of. Could you describe its "why" in one sentence? If not, how could the vision be clarified, and how might that improve the group?

2. What is the "how" of your group? How is your group—and how are you personally—working to achieve the vision? Does the "how" line up with the "why?"

3. What is the "what" of your group? What specific actions does your group take in line with your "how" to achieve your "why?" Do those actions contribute to the fulfillment of the group's purpose for existence, or are they distractions?

Chapter 15

WHAT DO YOU SEE?

am passionate about seeing you move in response to God's calling on your life. I can't wait to see what happens when you begin seeing his purposes in every moment, every word, every action of every day. God created you for a purpose. He made you for a reason. He gave you gifts, skills, and experiences that this world urgently needs.

When you and I, and the rest of his church, begin to think that way, our individual obedience becomes a movement that will fulfill God's promise from thousands of years ago. Through us—his people— God will bless all the families of the world.

I hope you see that, or at least glimpses of it. I hope you know that you weren't created just to exist. You were created to advance Jesus' movement on earth. You are part of a worldwide community that finds its local expression in your own church community, and God has created that community to literally bless every people group on this planet.

The Power of Alignment

Blessing is multiplied when we work together in alignment. Alignment is the arrangement of various parts into a cohesive, synergistic working relationship where each member does their share in achieving a common objective. Alignment happens when a team of people, from the leadership right through to the newest volunteer, are focused on the same goal and using the same strategies. Alignment is more than the sum of its parts because the parts are not working independently but as a unified team. This principle is found throughout Scripture:

> "Can two walk together, unless they are agreed?" (Amos 3:3 NKJV).

> "Two are better than one, because they have a good return for their labor" (Ecclesiastes 4:9 NIV).

> "Putting confidence in an unreliable person is like chewing with a toothache or walking on a broken foot" (Proverbs 25:19 NLT).

> "I appeal to you, brothers and sisters, in the name of our Lord Jesus Christ, that all of you agree with one another in what you say and that there be no divisions among you, but that you be perfectly united in mind and thought" (1 Corinthians 1:10 NIV).

Alignment is essential to living out our destiny and God's purposes for the church where he has planted us. As each individual part of a church, whether member, staff, or leader, finds our place in the body, recognizes our unique contribution, and aligns toward a common "why, how, and what," we accomplish together exponentially more than we ever could alone.

There are several key truths to understand here. I'll just summarize them briefly.

1. Alignment helps each of us find our unique place in the body of Christ so that we complement one another.

> For just as each of us has one body with many members, and these members do not all have the same function, so in Christ we, though many, form one body, and each member belongs to all the others. (Romans 12:4–5)

You and I are different from one another and from everyone else in the church. That is an essential ingredient to a healthy church! Homogenous churches, where people all strive to be carbon copies of one another, don't reflect the beauty of God's creation. They also lack the strength to handle the complexities of life. Alignment means we recognize our uniqueness and diversity, and we learn how to integrate those differences so that each of us plays the vital role God has created for us.

2. Alignment brings health to the body of Christ.

> Instead, we will speak the truth in love, growing in every way more and more like Christ, who is the head of his body, the church. He makes the whole body fit together perfectly. As each part does its own special work, it helps the other parts grow, so that the whole body is healthy and growing and full of love. (Ephesians 4:15-16 NLT)

I love the phrase "As each part does its own special work, it helps the other parts grow." Your growth in maturity and the talents you bring don't just help you and the community as a whole. They help the other individual members grow as well. I can't tell you how many times I've been challenged, encouraged, supported, and strengthened by another member of the body of Christ. We are part of one another, and our mutual growth strengthens each other continually.

3. Alignment happens on multiple levels.

> I urge you to live a life worthy of the calling you have received... So Christ himself gave the apostles, the prophets, the evangelists, the pastors and teachers, to equip his people for works of service, so that the body of Christ may be built up... Speaking the truth in love, we will grow to become in every respect the mature body of him who is the head, that is, Christ. From him

> the whole body, joined and held together by every supporting
> ligament, grows and builds itself up in love, as each part does
> its work. (Ephesians 4:1, 11–12, 15–16)

First and foremost, this means aligning yourself with God. Your alignment to his heart and revealed will for your life through Scripture forms the plumb line that helps ensure all other alignment is healthy. Secondly, align yourself with the church where God has planted you. That means you understand the vision of the church, love and serve the community around it, and are willing to support its work with your resources as God enables. If you are part of a church with a multi-site model, such as Mannahouse, this includes loving your church in its entirety as well as connecting in a meaningful way at one specific campus. Our campuses all share common values and vision, but each one is unique because of its location, leadership, and the members that make it up. Alignment means getting involved at your church location and using the talents and gifts God has given us to serve your local community while championing the region-wide vision God has given your church. My passion is that each individual would become a vibrant, vital member of a local church community who loves and serves its vision.

4. Alignment establishes mutual accountability.

> And let us consider how we may stir one another on to love
> and good deeds. (Hebrews 10:24)

When we have a truly healthy relationship with one another and we share a common vision, accountability becomes natural. I am not talking about some unhealthy, controlling approach to life. Domineering over one another is the antithesis of the way of Jesus; we are told to "submit to one another out of reverence for Christ' (Ephesians 5:21). I am talking about mutual encouragement, support, and the honesty that comes when we are truly open with one another. In that spirit of love and support, we are able to help one another stay on course.

5. Alignment brings clarity to our community's vision so that we are focused on the essentials rather than distracted by every perceived opportunity.

> If the trumpet does not sound a clear call, who will get ready for battle? (1 Corinthians 14:8)

Churches need to understand our "why, how, and what" in order to stay focused. Otherwise, we will chase every opportunity, respond to every need, and react to every threat to the detriment of our God-given purpose. We cannot do everything, so let's focus on doing the core things well, with an emphasis on health and sustainability. If we feel obligated to say yes to every opportunity that arises, we will either burn out or end up starting far more projects than we can possibly finish. Creativity and passion will slowly ebb as we rush around trying to do more than God ever called us to do in the first place. Alignment to God's purposes helps us slow down, focus, allow his creativity to flow through us, and ultimately achieve far more—and have more fun doing it!

6. Alignment eliminates personal agendas.

> I hope in the Lord Jesus to send Timothy to you soon, that I also may be cheered when I receive news about you. I have no one else like him, who will show genuine concern for your welfare. For everyone looks out for their own interests, not those of Jesus Christ. But you know that Timothy has proved himself, because as a son with his father he has served with me in the work of the gospel. (Philippians 2:19–22)

When we commit to do the same thing, it exposes anything that competes, even in our own souls. Rarely do we even realize we have a personal agenda. Our motives usually seem pure to ourselves, and—unsurprisingly—we tend to think our own ideas are really good. Alignment forces us to lay down those agendas for the good of the body and the glory of Christ. While that can be incredibly difficult, the process is valuable because it forces us to examine our own hearts. Why do we cling so tightly to some particular project, idea, or strategy? I've found in my own life that very often it's less about the thing itself and more about what it represents to me. Being willing to come into alignment with God and others in the church has helped me recognize ambition, pride, insecurities, and fear that God wants to deal with in my life.

7. Alignment releases supernatural anointing.

> How good and pleasant it is
> when God's people live together in unity!
> It is like precious oil poured on the head,
> running down on the beard,
> running down on Aaron's beard,
> down on the collar of his robe.
> It is as if the dew of Hermon
> were falling on Mount Zion.
> For there the Lord bestows his blessing,
> even life forevermore.
> (Psalm 133:1–3)

When we fully and completely align with heart and hand, heaven joins with us to break through barriers, release divine empowerment in the church, and add the Lord's favor and blessing to our work.

Our Righteous Cause

After significant nationwide and regional unrest, not to mention a global pandemic, I sat down to consider what the Lord was saying to our church. I've often started times like this with a list of things I'd like to see accomplished and called it vision. But this time, rather than writing a list of to-dos, I decided to write what I saw. Over the course of about six weeks, I wrote and rewrote a series of sentences beginning with "I see..." I wanted to imagine a movement of disciples in the Pacific Northwest. If we really lived up, in, and out, what would the church look like? If we broke the inertia and got unstuck, what would happen? What if we believed and acted on what is in this book?

Along with Michal and a group of trusted leaders on our team, I spent time praying and wondering. What did God want our church to look and feel like? We have lots of programs, staff who are passionate and hardworking, and whiteboards full of ideas for the future. But with all of our busyness, what are we building? Is it what God is calling us to be, or are we just mimicking others? God has given each of us—each person and each local church—a unique gift mix and a unique calling because he wants to use us to advance his kingdom in our sphere of influence. We needed to have a clear vision of why he had made us and what he wanted us to look like.

So we began to write, to re-write, and to refine. We finished with a series of statements that has become a manifesto of sorts for us (but not the cult kind), a document that envisions what God has called our church to be in the place where we are.

This is what I see when I pray over our congregation and our city. It is what gets me up in the morning, keeps me focused through distractions, and motivates me when times are rough. I include it here because I want to challenge you to believe for more than you can see with your natural eyes. If you are part of the church I lead, this is what we see! If you are part of another church, I hope this stirs you to clarify God's call on you and your team. We call it, "Our Righteous Cause."

I see a church that is an unstoppable movement of disciples, not a static religious institution. Its people know that advancing Jesus' movement will take all they've got.

I see a church known for its table-centered hospitality found in the way of Jesus—the one who loved them in their unloveliness and died for them in their sinfulness. They own their past mistakes and live a lifestyle of humility, surrender, and repentance.

I see a church known for its new sounds of presence-filled worship, sacrificial praise, and prophetic songs of deliverance—all overflowing from gratitude for second chances.

I see a church that is spiritually alive, moving in the power of the Holy Spirit—a people of prayer, fasting, expectation, miracles, holiness, and the fear of God. This church operates in spiritual gifts with boldness, accountability, and accuracy.

I see a church shaped by the truth and authority of God's Word, where the Bible is taught with relevance and compassion. The gospel is the best news, and this church can't wait to share it.

I see a church of diverse people who know there's room at the table for the gritty work of reconciliation and justice and where everyone's worth in Jesus is celebrated.

I see a church that thrives on the wisdom of the old and the energy of the young. It showcases a unified multicultural, multiethnic, and multigenerational identity to the world around them.

I see a church that pursues health and wholeness in God. Its people grieve, lament, forgive, heal, laugh, and have fun. They know how to work hard and rest well.

I see a church that engages the city's commerce, systems, and structures. It breaks the curse of poverty wherever it goes, continually advocating for justice and lifting people's heads to think, dream, and prosper in life.

I see a church where kids are loved and their caring discipleship is priority because the kingdom belongs to them. Students are championed as sons and daughters of God, and they are equipped to thrive amid cultural storms.

I see a church where leaders are equipped in character and skill and deployed into every part of society. Their work is sacred, and they seek to honor God in all they do.

I see a church full of groundbreaking innovators, artists, and marketplace leaders. New ideas and bold initiatives are common because God is creative and so are his people.

I see a church that celebrates each other equally whether married or single, and God's ideal of all relationships is lovingly held as the model and standard for human flourishing.

I see a church that breaks free from the lie of worldly success. Their minds are fixed on eternity, and they give their time, treasure, and talents as God leads and for his glory.

I see a church that sends its people to neighborhoods, cities, and nations. It shares its resources with other ministries and churches to strengthen leaders both near and far.

I see a church that stands together as one unified team, boldly living out God's eternal purpose, blessed by its legacy and embracing its destiny.

This is a cause that I am willing to commit to with my whole heart and life. I will leave Haran and journey through each stage toward the inheritance God has promised me. I will build altars, confront my fears, and move past my failures. I will join with the others God has brought alongside me, working together as a community of faith to advance Jesus' movement.

I believe this is the kind of church that honors God and loves people. It doesn't do this by being a "feel-good" community where no one is asked to sacrifice, grow, or change. I'm not interested in leading that kind of church. Yes, it would be comfortable. But Jesus is calling us to something much more exciting than comfort. He has given us a purpose that propels us forward, a common cause that unites us. Those who feel at home with us are those who yearn to respond to God's call to move.

What Do You See?

Jesus' movement is advancing worldwide, and you and I have a part to play in it. This requires movement of our own. We are made to move—created to respond to God's call on our lives with faith and passion. Advancing his movement is at the core of our "why."

That call is both high-invitation and high-challenge. It's not for the lukewarm or fainthearted. It's a call not just to modify our lives but to surrender them to Jesus and his mission. It's an invitation to join with him in both relationship and purpose. It is a call to discipleship. As we are discipled by Jesus and share that relationship with others, we become disciples making disciples.

What that looks like in practice is what I have been calling life at the table. We invite others into our lives. We show hospitality to those in our faith community and to those who are reluctant to darken the door of a church. We are vulnerable, honest, real, open, caring, empathetic, and loving. We see purpose in every single action of our day because advancing Jesus' movement is about loving the people we encounter in the same way Jesus did.

It's simple, actually. The deepest truths nearly always are. You are called by God. You don't have to be perfect; just be willing to obey. You don't have to know the destination; just be ready to say yes to the next step. You don't have to have a complex strategy to reach the world; just recognize that God's Spirit wants to infuse every part of your daily routine with purpose.

So, what do you see? What is God asking you today? How is he stirring your heart, and how is he asking you to respond? It will take faith, courage, and persistence. There will be stages of advancement and stages of trial. But it is worth it. Your life has a purpose, and discovering that purpose is a lifelong adventure.

You are made to move. You are part of Jesus' worldwide movement. You have been called, and now it's time to respond. It's an invitation and a challenge. And it's the most exciting life you could ever choose.

Questions for Reflection _____

1. How aligned are you with your church's vision and strategies? Are there ways you could become more aligned so that your gifts and talents contribute more effectively? What hindrances need to be overcome for that to happen?

2. "Our Righteous Cause" lists sixteen aspects of Mannahouse's vision for our future. Whether you are part of Mannahouse or not, some or all of these probably resonate with you, while others are more challenging. Which ones excite you most? Which ones are you hesitant about, and why?

3. What areas is God calling you personally to move in? What dream or challenge is he calling you toward? What are your fears about it? What is the first step of obedience, the one he's asking you to take today? Will you take it?

CONCLUSION

My father was born into a poor farming community in the mountains of North Carolina. While his mother was a believer, he didn't have a relationship with Jesus. After a time of serving in the military, he married my mother who he met at a burger bar just outside the little town of Tuckaseegee. A lack of work in that part of the US in a post-depression time led them to pioneer a new life on the West Coast as a way to support themselves and their first soon to be born son.

After some years of ups and downs, my mom became part of a small Pentecostal church. She found a community of faithful disciples who took her in and began to not only provide her with encouragement, but taught her the truths of God's Word. Later, my dad had an encounter with Jesus sitting on his bedside on a Sunday morning while my mom was in church. He describes the moment as electricity touching the top of his head and shooting through his entire body. Interestingly from that moment on, several habits and addictions fell by the wayside. He was truly baptized by the Holy Spirit and fire.

Dad would eventually join my mom in church, and a man named Lloyd Crumb began to disciple my dad. Sitting at my parent's table, often until midnight, this man shared words that were like life to my dad's soul. I asked my dad how it all started and he said that one day Lloyd pulled him aside at a Sunday service and said, "I knew when you walked into church that if someone didn't teach you the Word, you'd go back to all your rough coworkers and lose your faith." He also told him that "sometimes those preachers talk over everyone's head and you just need the simple truth of the Word."

Lloyd went to my parents' house multiple times a week and sat with my dad for hours to disciple him. The table they sat at is still in my dad's dining room. Just last week, literally seven days ago from when I'm writing these words, I sat at the same table, and we had a family meeting to talk about my dad's medical journey, his end of life plan, and how we'd handle his estate. He's eighty-seven years old and just isn't as quick and sharp as he used to be. When he dies, there will be a major gap in my life. But my mom, who died just over three years ago, will be celebrating and will welcome him to his eternal reward, no doubt!

As we sat there talking as a family, one thing was for certain. My dad loves Jesus. And his family loves Jesus. And it struck me again: it all started at that very table.

A passion for the pervasive movement of Jesus on the earth today consumes me. And I see it emerging in the Pacific Northwest and around the world. While it's true that we live in dark times and evil persists, I cannot and will not lose heart. The city where I pastor is filled with every form of evil imaginable. It is one of the darkest on the West Coast. What others see as a reason to flee, I see as an opportunity. I will MOVE closer to God, closer to each other, and closer to the world around me.

Ultimately, I suppose that the motor in me comes from the conviction that the church will be victorious and will carry out the eternal purpose and plan of God. Light will overshadow darkness and the glory of God will cover the entire earth. The promise from God himself in Genesis 3:15 stirs my heart daily: "He shall bruise your head, and you shall bruise his heel" (NKJV). If that were not enough, I read Jesus' declaration found in Matthew 16:18, which says, "On this rock I will build my church, and the gates of hell shall not prevail against it" (ESV), and I find myself even more emboldened to join Jesus in what he's doing. And again, I find myself strengthened even more by recalling moments where I heard the founder of the church I pastor, Dick Iverson, declare Numbers 14:21. "But truly, as I live, all the earth shall be filled with the glory of the LORD..." (NKJV).

My prayer for you is that you find a community where you can do life at the table. At that table, I pray that you are vulnerable, that you can share your life and brokenness with others and experience the same. As you do, may you become a disciple who makes disciples. Then together, we will advance Jesus' movement.

Appendix

MOVE

OUR DISCIPLESHIP MODEL

M
annahouse is a movement of disciples, campuses, schools, and churches in the Pacific Northwest. Our passion is that every individual who we interact with would be swept into the momentum of a tribe of people from all over the region who are on the move, closer to God, closer to each other, and closer to the world around them.

MOVE describes our discipleship model. If you are part of our local church, this will help you understand why we do what we do—and how you can be part. If you are a member of another church, you are welcome to use this as a model for your own community to develop intentional ways to equip your church members.

Firsts are important, especially in Scripture. First word usage, a person's arrival into the biblical narrative, or the first time a principle is taught; all these bear critical and important details that will be necessary to consider as the study of the whole of Scripture unfolds.

Before Jesus ever launched miracle ministry, he began assembling a ragged band of disciples—in fact, after his temptation in the wilderness, besides a quick preaching assignment on repentance, his first act was to call two men to move. "Jesus called out to them, 'Come, follow me, and I will show you how to fish for people!'" (Matthew 4:19 NLT)

> Jesus called them UP—closer to God
> Jesus called them IN—closer to each other
> Jesus sent them OUT—closer to the world around them

While training and discipleship in the American church has been primarily linear, in the East, it's circular. One has a start and an end, the other is never-ending. It's our belief that Jesus was calling these two disciples into a lifetime journey of movement. It would be "here a little and there a little" (Isaiah 28:10 NASB).

The MOVE Discipleship Pathway

The MOVE Discipleship Pathway is a combination of classes, groups, and meetings developed to help you initiate and sustain a lifetime of movement that is UP, IN, and OUT.

Like most things, the material by itself is not the sole indicator of effectiveness—you'll get out of it what you put into it. The pathway we've laid out will provide a lot of opportunities to learn, practice, discover your gifts, and develop skills to help others. But ultimately, the responsibility is yours to obey God and step out in faith. We're excited to help you, if you are willing to move!

We ask everyone to begin their journey at Mannahouse at Starting Point. This is the specific point in your journey where you can decide to become a serving member of the Mannahouse church family. The other three steps—Freedom, Foundations, and Disciple Maker's Workshop—can be taken at any point in your journey.

1. Starting Point

Starting Point is a one-day small group experience that happens during a weekend church service. It is led by a pastoral leader on the team and covers topics such as salvation, water baptism, the baptism of the Holy Spirit, and commitment to the local church. It will help you understand the core values of our community and how you can be a part of that. After the class, a member of our pastoral staff will meet with you personally to discuss the best next steps for you.

2. Freedom

Freedom is a twelve-session small group that dives deep into Christ's plan for setting every believer free from their past and empowering them to walk in daily freedom by the power of the Holy Spirit. The group sessions conclude with a weekend encounter with everyone across the church who went through Freedom in that group season. We have found it to be an incredibly powerful way for people to break free of past hurts, habits, addictions, and negative thought patterns so they can learn to move forward with new joy and peace.

3. Foundations

Foundations is a twelve-week small group that guides individuals to discover what the Bible says about several core doctrines that, when applied to life, will accelerate discipleship. Topics such as sin, repentance, church, finances, forgiveness, and more are covered. Studying these truths is a foundational part of understanding how Jesus' love and truth transform every area of our lives.

4. Disciple Maker's Workshop

Disciple Maker's Workshop is a one-day intensive that inspires disciples to live a lifetime journey on the move and to be part of advancing Jesus' movement by making disciples, too. It's the call of every disciple to make disciples, but that can sound daunting. It doesn't need to! This time spent together will equip and commission you to be right in the middle of advancing Jesus' movement.

ENDNOTES

1   Anna Baluch, "Average PTO In The US & Other PTO Statistics (2024)" Forbes, March 30, 2023, https://www.forbes.com/advisor/business/pto-statistics/.

2   "Literary Styles," How to Read the Bible Series, June 22, 2017, Bible Project, https://bibleproject.com/explore/video/literary-styles-bible/#:~:text=Narrative%20%5B00%3A37%2D02,33%20percent%20of%20the%20Bible.

3   "Our Epidemic of Loneliness and Social Isolation, 2023: The U.S. Surgeon General's Advisory on the Healing Effects of Social Connection and Community, https://www.hhs.gov/sites/default/files/surgeon-general-social-connection-advisory.pdf (accessed 9/9/23).

4   Dan Witters, "Loneliness in US Subsides from Pandemic High," Gallup, April 4, 2023, https://news.gallup.com/poll/473057/loneliness-subsides-pandemic-high.aspx.

5   Brenda Euland, "Tell Me More," Ladies' Home Journal, 1941 (cited by Quote Investigator, https://quoteinvestigator.com/2014/06/13/listen/).

6   "Gottman-Rapoport Intervention," https://static1.squarespace.com/static/55bbdcf9e4b0c50a1d8402c7/t/5bc4cf210d92979df6551 4b5/1539624737634/Gottman+Rapoport.pdf (accessed May 27, 2024).

7   Mike Breen, "Why the Missional Movement Will Fail," Verge Network Blog, https://vergenetwork.org/2011/09/14/mike-breen-why-the-missional-movement-will-fail/ (accessed May 27, 2024).

8   Verlon Fosner, "The Historic Dinner Church," Dinner Church Collective, 11, freshexpressions.org.

9   Ibid, p.12,13

10   David Augsberger, "Caring Enough to Hear and Be Heard: How to Hear and Be Heard in Equal Communication" (Baker Pub: 1982).

11   "Who Was Abraham and Where Did He Come From?" Bet Yeshurun Messianic Community, https://www.messianics.us/bible-history/who-was-abraham.html (accessed May 27, 2024).

12   C.S. Lewis, The Four Loves (London: Geoffrey Bles, 1960), online version by Project Gutenberg Canada, https://gutenberg.ca/ebooks/lewiscs-fourloves/lewiscs-fourloves-00-h.html.

13   Simona Kitanovska, "Younger Americans Most Likely to Feel Unsafe on a Daily Basis: Poll," Newsweek.com, July 28, 2022, https://www.newsweek.com/young-americans-most-likely-feel-unsafe-daily-basis-poll-1728660.

14   Edith Anne Stewart, "The life of St. Francis Xavier: evangelist, explorer, mystic (Headley Bro. Publishers: 1917), 97

15   Pew Research Group, "Geographical Distribution of Religious Groups," December 18, 2012, https://www.pewresearch.org/religion/2012/12/18/global-religious-landscape-exec/.

ACKNOWLEDGMENTS

Mariah, Judah, and Noah Corbin. Thank you for faithfully pursuing God's will in your own lives. Watching you move closer to God and love each other is my absolute greatest joy.

My dad and mom, Phil and Nancy Corbin. These pioneers carved a life out of nothing, and with the Lord's guidance they built an eternal legacy through their family. I am forever grateful for the bold and tenacious way they followed God and imparted faith to the next generation.

My siblings Angela, Jerry, and Frank, I want to offer my thanks and deep appreciation for your continual encouragement, love, and support.

Dick and Edie Iverson, Frank and Sharon Damazio, Dave and Fran Huebert, Lew and Marion Peterson, Marc and Susan Estes, Bill and Joanne Scheidler, Jack and Libby Louman, Lanny and Joanne Hubbard, Larry and Lynda Asplund, Ken and Glenda Malmin, Steve and Beth Cole, Jim and Laura Davis, Bob and Sharon Wagar, and Dave and Alynne Shinness were leaders who impacted our lives in ways we cannot describe.

The people of Life Center, the church my wife and I pioneered in our early married years, will forever be my heroes. They saw what could be, rallied to the cause, stood fast in dark times, and walked in the fulfillment of God's prophetic promises. We learned and grew together, and our lives will never be the same.

I can't say enough about the congregation and team I lead at Mannahouse. You inspire me by your faith and challenge me by your commitment to God and his purposes. Our best days are ahead!

And with all that I am, I'm grateful to Jesus who invited me to be his disciple and to advance his movement.

Let's move!

ABOUT THE AUTHOR

Derrill and Michal Corbin are the lead pastors of Mannahouse, a mult-site church based in Portland, Oregon. Derrill and Michal met at Portland Bible College and were married soon after graduating. They served on the church staff under Dick and Edie Iverson and then Frank and Sharon Damazio. In 1997, they planted a church in the Pacific Northwest, which they pastored and lead for sixteen years, developing it into a thriving multi-site church. In 2013, they returned to Mannahouse (formerly known as City Bible Church) where they now serve.

Besides their pastoring roles, Derrill is chancellor of PBC, and Michal owns and operates her own fitness studio, is very active in the community, and serves on a variety of teams in the church. Derrill has a Bachelor of Theology degree from PBC and a Masters of Sacred Studies degree from Christian Life School of Theology (CLST).

Derrill and Michal are known for their personal and creative leadership and insightful communication. They are dedicated to discipling people into a movement that impacts people everywhere. They reside in Camas, Washington with their three children: Mariah, Judah, and Noah.